An Adven in Mysticism

Featuring:
The Gospel According to "I Am"

By Don Mardak

CTE Publications - New Berlin, WI

An
Adventure
in
Mysticism

Dedicated to
All Seekers of Truth

Part One

The Adventure

(Awakening & Awareness)

INTRODUCTION

There is a spiritual "Something"—a Divine Presence—lying dormant in each one of us. When we awaken to this Presence, it becomes an activity of grace operating at the center of our being and, ultimately, will lead us to our own spiritual destiny.

Living as the "man of earth," our human experience is centered in a physical body that is functioning in a three-dimensional universe. This materialistic concept of existence has been ingrained in us since our birth, and *our acceptance* of this concept has subjected us to a lifetime of limitation. We live under laws of matter, laws of medicine, laws of heredity and economics, and, most important, we are subject to the law of the calendar.

At some point in our experience, however, we may cross paths with a person of elevated mystical consciousness. This encounter, which could involve a personal meeting or may merely be the discovery of a book on spiritual wisdom, awakens a response in us, and that Something within begins to stir.

At first, we are introduced to a few new concepts about the nature of our existence. As our initial curiosity evolves into a gradual acceptance of these principles, our thirst for knowledge grows, and we begin to realize that, like the Apostle Paul, we have been seeing our world "through a glass darkly."

Our consciousness then enters a transcendental phase in which its horizons are expanding. As this occurs, our personal point-of-reference no longer is a mere physical body. Instead, we gain some awareness of our true identity and of our relationship to the Source of all life.

Through this transcendental consciousness, we discover the purity and perfection of a fourth-dimensional, spiritual state of being. In this fourth-dimensional state, we attain conscious union with God and then can honestly say with Paul, "I live, yet not I, but Christ liveth in me."

As we chart our journey from sense to Soul, we soon realize that, while outwardly our life has undergone a remarkable transition, in reality nothing has changed. It is not that our consciousness has actually grown from finite limitation to infinity. Rather, we have achieved a new, higher level of awareness. We have become aware of the infinite nature of our being and of that which already Is: "I AM That I AM."

The Master Christian has told us that "Strait is the gate, and narrow is the way, which leadeth unto life." And we are not given much encouragement by the price he has asked us to pay: "Leave your nets" and "Call no man your Father upon the earth." Yet when we are motivated by that activity of grace within us, we cannot refuse to set aside our personal desires and human relationships so that we may follow that "strait and narrow way."

This is the story of one man's spiritual awakening and his ultimate search for Truth.

Chapter One

If the Christ appeared on earth today, would this divine coincidence of God and man be recognized and accepted in the hearts and minds of the people of this age any more than it was two thousand years ago? If someone living today was led to the inescapable conclusion that, in his true identity, he actually is the Son of God, would anyone else perceive that same divinity?

While I cannot answer those questions with an absolute certainty, there is a related fact of which I am convinced: The individual enlightened consciousness that previously appeared on earth as a Gautama, as a Shankara, as a Jesus, John or Paul, is still alive and functioning. And, if any of those illumined beings were to reincarnate in our time, they would carry with them the attained wisdom and spiritual intuition of their previous lives.

I truly believe that, at any given moment, each one of us represents the sum total of our past experiences. But that conclusion raises a series of additional intriguing questions: Did all those past experiences necessarily occur during just this present lifetime? Are there not other planes of consciousness—other realms of existence—to which we have access? Can life itself not be depicted, as it is in certain Eastern philosophies, as a circle, without beginning or ending? And, based on that premise, can we not then think of our own present life-experience as existing between a set of parentheses superimposed on that circle, i.e., "a parenthesis in eternity"?

Because I have found my answers to most of these questions, I am sharing my story with you in the hope that it will lead you to your own personal search for Truth, thus enabling you to also find your answers. But to preface my story, I would like to interject a few thoughts concerning the formative years in the life of Christ Jesus—those years that contributed to the ultimate development of his spiritual consciousness.

The four gospels, which record the life and ministry of the Master, provide little information about his early experiences. We are told of the episode in Jerusalem when, at the age of twelve, he became separated from his parents and appeared to be lost, only to be discovered later discussing spiritual truth with the doctors in the temple. But after that incident, we have no record of Jesus' activities until the Bible narratives pick up his story when he is approximately thirty years old and is about to be baptized in the River Jordan by John the Baptist.

What took place during the unrecorded eighteen years of the Master's life? What events molded his inquisitive mind?

Did he merely stay near his parents' home in Nazareth, working at his father's side, developing the skills of his chosen carpenter's trade? Did he spend his free time with the local rabbi, studying the Torah and imbibing the strict letter of the Hebraic law which he so profoundly reinterpreted during his ministry? Or, as some Bible scholars suggest, did Jesus actually travel to far-away places, meeting illumined teachers of spiritual wisdom and gaining the conviction that ultimately led him to the remarkable and controversial conclusion that, indeed, he was the Christ, the only begotten son of God?

For centuries, rumors and speculative theories on this subject have abounded. Some scholars claim that Jesus spent several years in India, or possibly in the British Isles. Others believe that he became a member of the ascetic Essene sect of Jews. But whatever his background and training during those "missing eighteen years," this spiritually awakened Hebrew did, in fact, discover his own true identity as the Christ of God, and that discovery led him to the understanding that that same divinity exists in every man. His final prayer was: "That they all may be one; as Thou, Father, art in me, and I in Thee, that they also may be one in us: I in them, and Thou in me, that they may be made perfect in one."

If, in truth, we all are one with the Father, then there is a divine Presence functioning within each of us. That is the great spiritual secret that has been revealed by all the illumined mystics of the past. Yet throughout the entire recorded history of mankind, only a select few individuals have actually discovered the real, esoteric meaning of life and, then, through the ordination of the Spirit, were able to contribute to the uplifting, or spiritualization, of human consciousness.

As these enlightened men and women discovered absolute Truth for themselves, they realized that, in accordance with the Apostle Paul's exhortation, the "old man" in them had died, and a "new man" had been born of the Spirit.

In a few isolated cases, their mystical initiation was a very sudden, instantaneous experience: one of the most noteworthy examples being Saul of Tarsus encountering the risen Christ on the road to Damascus. For others, illumination came more slowly and was the gradual result of a series of spiritual unfoldments. But in spite of the seemingly miraculous nature of the events surrounding the lives of many religious notables of the past, spiritual illumination, or enlightenment, is the ultimate destiny of each one of us. However, for most of us this may be an unlikely and arduous undertaking unless, somehow, we are motivated by the Spirit. Fortunately, there is an activity of grace functioning within each of us, and if we are receptive to it, this grace of God will lead us into places and circumstances that will provide many opportunities for our introduction to mystical principles.

Through this grace of God within me, I, too, have become a seeker after Truth. Yet, there was nothing in my early background to indicate that I eventually would follow such a course. As with most of us, my human history is of no real significance. The years before my spiritual awakening can be capsulized in a few short paragraphs.

I was born and raised in a suburb of Chicago, Illinois. My parents were of traditional Midwest stock and could have been classified as white, Anglo-Saxon Protestants who adhered to the Judeo-Christian work ethic. My father was a carpenter by trade, having served a full apprenticeship after graduating from high school. My mother was two years younger than my father. In fact, she was just fifteen years old when they met—he, the starting left halfback on the school's football team, and she, a freshman addition to the cheerleading squad. They had their first unchaperoned date a year later when he was a high school senior. Apparently, theirs was a relationship sealed in heaven, because after that first evening together, neither of them ever again dated anyone else. They were married shortly after Mom's graduation, and I was born two years later, at which time she gave up her part-time job as a bookkeeper to become a full-time housewife and mother.

While my father's basic trade was carpentry, he also was extremely knowledgable about all mechanical and electrical machinery, having a natural gift for understanding the way things work. He virtually was a mechanical engineer, even though he had no degrees or formal engineering training. Combining this unique, inborn ability with a strong entrepreneurial drive, he was able to establish his own machine-tool design company while he still was a very young man. That small business provided our family with a reasonably comfortable existence, although we occasionally experienced a financial setback whenever the national economy went into one of its periodic recessions.

We were not an overly religious family, but my parents did attend worship services fairly regularly at a neighborhood Protestant church. From the time I was six years old, I was enrolled in Sunday school and attended classes about half the time.

Like most people, I had a few early educational experiences that will always stand out in my memory. I vividly remember the first time my Sunday school teacher announced that I was "created in the image and likeness of God."

What a revelation! I now knew what God looked like.

After glancing down at my body, I thought, "Gee . . . God has two arms and two legs." This initial reaction, which I later discovered was very common among my peers, produced a concept of God that was to remain with me for several years. But in formulating this concept, I had used faulty human logic. Instead of reasoning from cause to effect, I, like much of mankind, reversed the process. Starting from the standpoint of an effect (my own physical body), I reasoned backward to deduce the Cause (God); thereby "creating" my God in the image and likeness of man.

Another point that kept my mind working overtime was the concept of eternity. In Sunday school, I was taught that "God always was and always will be." My young psyche could accept God's existence now, along with the possibility that He would continue to exist. But I couldn't grasp the concept of no beginning, i.e., "God always was. . . ."

In my subsequent search for Truth, both of these points—the nature of God and the concept of eternity—would eventually be clarified for me. Yet aside from those two questions and a few moderately "intellectual discussions" with my childhood friends, there was nothing in my early experiences that could foretell the deep quest for spiritual wisdom that soon was to be awakened in me.

My introduction to mysticism took place when I was just twelve years old. During that summer recess from school, my parents and I had decided to take a trip to the Holy Land. Though the journey was to be an educational vacation for our family, it would be subsidized in part by my father's business affiliations. One of his major suppliers was quite active in the Middle East, and the marketing people of that company had asked him to conduct several meetings for them and call on a few of their clients in the area. However, even though the three of us had spent a number of weeks anxiously preparing for the vacation, none of us could have anticipated the mystical adventure that was awaiting me on those ancient streets once traversed by Jesus, Peter, John and Paul.

The day of our departure was a warm Saturday in August. We left Chicago that afternoon, had a brief refueling stopover in Paris, and arrived early Sunday at Israel's Ben Gurion airport. This was followed by a tedious customs check and then a very slow bus ride to the heart of Tel Aviv. Fortunately, the check-in process at our hotel was reasonably expeditious, and we spent the rest of that day becoming acclimated to our new surroundings.

Using our hotel in Tel Aviv as a base, we participated in several historical tours during our first week in Israel. One overnight tour took us to the coastal town of Haifa and then to Nazareth, the boyhood home of Jesus. We also visited Tiberius and Capernaum on the Sea of Galilee. On another excursion, we viewed the ancient city of Beersheba and travelled along the northern edge of the Negev Desert to Sodom and the Dead Sea. While there is much spiritual significance attributed to those historical landmarks, we had little contact with any of the contemporary residents and, for that reason, never became intimately involved with the area.

The following Sunday, we took the scenic train ride from Tel Aviv to Jerusalem and checked into the King David Hotel. After a few days of total relaxation in and around the hotel, we decided to participate in a guided tour of the Old City section of Jerusalem. Though this was somewhat a last-minute decision—the tour was scheduled for nine o'clock the next morning—the concierge at our hotel claimed that there were plenty of seats available. So at ten minutes before nine a.m. on Wednesday, my parents and I leisurely strolled down to the lobby of the King David Hotel. Five minutes later, under the unrelenting rays of a torrid desert sun, two dusty old khaki-colored buses pulled up to the front entrance of the hotel. Almost simultaneously, an extremely large group of anxious tourists, seemingly coming from all directions, began gathering in the lobby. Taken aback by the rapidly growing assembly, my father made some disparaging comment about the sales agents obviously overbooking this tour. He assumed that there was no way for that many people to fit into those rather small buses. But our two multi-lingual tour guides were not to be denied, as they systematically crammed all of us into the drab vehicles.

At first glance, these chartered buses appeared to be surplus World War II relics. Then, as we were squeezed into our seats, an ominous feeling came over me concerning the wartime function of these vehicles. I sensed that they once may have been used to transport panic-stricken hordes of Semitic people who were fleeing from their homes under the ferocious onslaught of Field Marshall Rommel's desert legions. Nevertheless, after our group was fully assembled in the buses, we began our slow, uncomfortable drive to the Old City. Arriving there, our first stop was at the Wailing Wall, the only remnant of the walls that once had surrounded Solomon's great temple. Then, starting near Saint Stephen's gate, we followed the Via Dolorosa to Golgotha.

According to tradition, this was the path taken by Jesus from the place where he was condemned to the scene of his crucifixion. We then toured the famous Church of the Holy Sepulchre which stands on Golgotha. Leaving the church, we retraced our steps down the Via Dolorosa, slowly walking the several blocks to our waiting tour buses.

As our large contingent was wandering through the crowded street, my attention was diverted to a small group of people just off the main road. From my vantage point, they seemed to be concluding some type of informal meeting or lecture. As they began dispersing from the area, two women left the group and walked past me. Though each of their faces was partially covered by a yashmak, the traditional Moslem veil, I observed in their eyes a look of peace and contentment that I had never seen before. Slowly I began drifting toward their meeting place as others were walking off in all directions. By the time I arrived, no one remained except a bearded old man sitting quietly on the edge of a low stone wall. His eyes were closed, but I could feel something special, a kind of peace, or spiritual presence, in the atmosphere.

After I had been standing there silently for a few moments, the old man gently opened his eyes. I saw in them that same glow of peace and contentment that I had recognized earlier in the two women. He smiled softly, and I slowly approached him. With his craggy, wrinkled features and sun-drenched, weathered skin, he appeared to be at least one hundred years old. If my schoolmates had been with me, the sight of this strange-looking man would have terrorized us, and more than likely we would have poked fun at him or run away in an open display of mock fright. But instead of reacting in those childish ways, I felt compelled to speak to him.

"Good afternoon. My name is Eric."

For a moment, he seemed surprised by my sudden intrusion, but then he replied, "And I am Nehemiah."

After a brief period of silence, I asked, "What was taking place here a few moments ago? What were all those people doing here?"

He smiled enthusiastically, and as he did so, his face came alive and he seemed to lose forty years off his age.

"We were listening to the Master Shimahn, who is visiting here from Tibet."

"Wow . . . Tibet!" I shouted. "Isn't that the country that's cut off from the whole world, way up there in the Himalayan Mountains?"

"Yes!"

"But what's he doing here in Jerusalem?"

"He is teaching us . . . revealing the mystical secret of the true meaning of our existence. He is guiding us on the path to ultimate reality."

Those words sounded most impressive to my young ears: "true meaning of our existence" . . . "ultimate reality".... But his speaking in such terms tended to contradict the ethnic appearance of this seemingly wise old man. He looked exactly like some of the Biblical characters portrayed in the epic motion pictures that were filmed in his native land. In fact, he could have been cast most authentically as one of the renowned Hebrew Patriarchs. Yet, I was having difficulty reconciling the old man's demeanor with the terminology he used when he described the teaching of his Master from Tibet.

I then asked, "Uh, Mr. Nehemiah . . . um . . . aren't you Jewish, or an Arab?"

"Please call me Nehemiah," he replied. "As you might suspect, I once was a follower of the Hebrew teachings of our fathers: Abraham, Isaac, Jacob and Moses."

"But weren't those two ladies I just passed Moslems?"

"Yes! And if you had come earlier, you also would have seen some who call themselves Christians, as well as two Buddhists, several Hindus and even one follower of Confucius."

I responded, "But those philosophies are all so different. . . . How can one teacher appeal to all of them?"

Nehemiah then rose to his feet, and I was surprised by his apparent strength and stature. He stood at least six-feet-three-inches tall. Gazing into my eyes, he said:

"There is only one basic Truth. All men will eventually recognize that fact. . . . Now if you will excuse me, Eric, I must visit someone."

"You're leaving. . . ? Must you go so soon, Nehemiah? When is Shimahn going to speak again?"

"Oh, I believe he will be lecturing in Cairo next Tuesday."

"In Cairo. . . ? Next Tuesday. . . ? But we're going back to America on Saturday!"

I was quite disappointed that I wouldn't have an opportunity to hear this master from the Far East. To my recollection, I had never before been interested in such matters, but my curiosity had been aroused, and something inside of me had awakened a great desire to be near him. I then asked:

"Isn't there some way I could meet with Shimahn? Couldn't you take me to him?"

"I think not, Eric. He is very busy at this time."

"Please, Nehemiah . . . I'll be going back to Chicago, and he'll be in Tibet. Our paths may never cross again."

"I am sorry, Eric, but do not be concerned. . . . You are a very young boy. You will find your true teacher when the time is right. Goodbye, Eric."

And with that statement, he turned quickly and walked off down the street. His gait was rapid and his strides were long; he moved like a man in the prime of his life. As Nehemiah turned the corner, I found myself running after him. Just as I reached that intersection, I saw him enter a doorway some distance down the road. I ran to the entrance, hoping to gain a final glimpse of my new-found friend, but to my dismay the door was tightly closed. However, a few feet to the left of the door, near the bottom of the wall, I noticed an open window that offered a view of a rather dark, sparsely furnished lower room. Inside, I saw an olive-skinned man, dressed in a white linen tunic and slacks, sitting in a somewhat relaxed lotus position. His eyes were closed in meditation, and his hands were folded gently in his lap. Facing him across the room were two women and another man, all sitting with their eyes closed. There seemed to be a great peace emanating from the room. Those inside were totally oblivious to the constant hum of noise from the busy market several blocks away and to the sounds of the local villagers passing by on foot or riding donkeys. Naturally, I didn't want to disturb the people in the room, so I just sat quietly outside the window. Sitting there, I felt a strange compulsion to close my eyes to see if I could feel the peacefulness they obviously were experiencing.

A short time later, I was aroused from my attempted meditation by a gentle stirring in the room. All four people had opened their eyes, and the three visitors were bidding goodbye to the man in white. I could barely hear them, but they seemed to be speaking a language other than English. As the people left, Nehemiah entered the room. He and the other man began conversing, but they, too, were speaking in a foreign language. I wondered if the man in white might be the Master Shimahn. Just at that moment, a horse pulling a cart in the street was frightened by a small animal that had crossed its path. As the horse reared up and neighed, the commotion in the street attracted the attention of the two men in the room. They looked up, and Nehemiah saw me kneeling at the corner of the window.

"Eric!" he shouted. "How long have you been up there?"

Nehemiah then said something to the other man, who smiled and made a gentle waving motion with his right hand. Nehemiah left the room, and a brief moment later the door next to me opened, as I heard the old Hebrew's voice say:

"Well, young man, you certainly are persistent. Come inside with me!"

I moved to the door and followed him down the steps. As we entered the room, the man in white extended his hand, smiling.

Nehemiah introduced us: "Eric, meet Shimahn . . . Shimahn, this is my new friend Eric."

"How do you do, Eric?" he said in perfect English with just a trace of a British accent.

"Hello, Mr. Shimahn," I replied, shaking his hand.

His skin was smooth, and his handshake was gentle but not delicate, firm but not overpowering. I looked down at his hands. The fingers were slender and long, the kind you might expect to see on a concert pianist or, possibly, on a brain surgeon. I then looked back up into his face. I think I'll remember Shimahn's eyes as long as I live. They were dark—a very dark brown, almost black. And when he looked at me, it seemed that he was not looking *at* me, but *through* me, penetrating to the very depths of my soul. In fact, for just an instant, I thought I was slipping into a hypnotic trance under the intensity of his probing eyes. But then, suddenly, my entire being was permeated by a profoundly intuitive sensation of recognition. I felt that I had met this man before. And, for just a flickering moment, his gaze broke as I sensed a reciprocal response in him. But before I could speak about my newly discovered capacity of extrasensory perception, Shimahn said:

"Eric, Nehemiah tells me that you wanted to meet with me. How can I be of service to you?"

I stood there in silence, staring at him, unable to speak. I couldn't answer. . . . Why was I there?

Something inside of me had motivated me to come. But how do you stand before one of the world's great spiritual teachers, a master from the Himalayas, and ask the kinds of questions that are so prevalent in the mind of a twelve-year-old?

Shimahn smiled, glancing briefly at Nehemiah. I felt a little foolish, but Shimahn didn't allow me to feel outwardly embarrassed.

Sensing my disconcertion, he then said, "Nehemiah and I were just going to meditate for a short while. Why don't you join us and we'll talk later." Shimahn escorted me to a chair and said, "Sit here, Eric. . . . Just sit comfortably and close your eyes."

I followed his instructions, and after a few moments of silence, this Tibetan master began to speak:

"God is Infinite. . . . There is only one all-inclusive Being, one immortal, eternal Life which we have named God." He paused for a moment and then said: "That one universal Life is the life of each of us in this room and is the life of every person who has ever appeared on this earth. Let us take a moment to contemplate this extraordinary Truth: The Life that is God is individually expressed as my life. Therefore, 'I and my Father are One' ... I and my Father are One. . . ."

And then Shimahn stopped speaking. With my eyes still closed, I tried to ponder what he had said: "God is my life . . . I and my Father are One." But my mind seemed to stop functioning. It was almost as if I had been drawn into a complete vacuum in which my mind wanted to rest and not think thoughts. I could not measure the time that passed. It seemed like a few minutes, but it may have been as little as thirty seconds or as long as a half hour. Then Shimahn spoke again:

"Thank you, Eric. That was a most peaceful meditation. I can feel that you are very receptive."

"Receptive to what?" I wondered. I had to agree that I certainly felt a deep sense of peace. In fact, I was so relaxed that I could easily have gone to sleep.

Shimahn then asked, "Now can we answer any questions for you, Eric?"

Questions? My head was exploding with questions! Trying to find the proper words, I haltingly asked:

"Umm . . . well . . . when we had our eyes closed, you mentioned a few things about God, and then you said, 'I and my Father are One.' Didn't Jesus say that in the Bible? Could you explain what you meant by that?"

"Well, Eric, most of the eminent spiritual revelators— Krishna, Moses, Shankara, Lao Tze, Isaiah, Christ Jesus, and many other mystics who have followed them—have all given us the same basic message. That message is first and foremost: that God is infinite . . . omnipresent, omnipotent and omniscient."

"Heck, Shimahn, that's nothing new. I learned all that in my Sunday school. I've heard all those words like 'omnipotent' before."

"Ah, yes, Eric . . . so you have. Most religions use those words. But more often than not, those teachings don't follow the words through to their logical conclusions. Do you understand what 'omnipotent' means?"

"Not really! I . . . uh . . . I think my teacher said it's something like 'all-powerful'."

"That is correct, Eric. 'Omni' is the Latin word meaning 'all'. All-potent . . . omnipotent . . . all-power. But then if we accept that basic premise, we must follow with the question: How can a God who is omnipotent allow any opposing power?"

"Do you mean like the Devil?"

"Right! An all-powerful, omnipotent God does not share His power with anyone or anything. . . . And as another example, how can we have an infinite, omnipresent Creator—which means God is everywhere and fills all space—and then accept the existence of anything separate from God? In other words, nothing exists outside of the God-Consciousness."

"Do you mean to say that I don't exist?"

"Aha!!! Now you're thinking, Eric. Of course you do. Your senses testify to your existence. You are conscious of that fact. But my question to you is: Do you have existence separate and apart from God?"

"I don't know!"

"Oh, but you really do know the answer. You just haven't spent much time thinking about it. If we accept God as infinite and omnipresent (the only Presence), then everything that exists must actually be God appearing in some particular form . . . and that includes you and me. Each of us is an individualized expression of God's Own Being. That is why we can say with the Master: 'I and my Father are One.'"

By that time my head was spinning. Shimahn was using quite a few big words that my twelve-year-old mentality had never heard before. Yet, I sensed a certain logic in what he was saying—a logic that I couldn't refute. But I wondered how these concepts would stand up in the light of the Scriptures and other philosophies. I asked Shimahn about this.

"It's all there, Eric," he said. "Your Christian Bible has all these facts. You see, the Bible, as you know it, was written over a period of many years by a number of different people. Each author was writing for a specific group of people during his particular time in history. Much of what is chronicled there is influenced by the traditions, prejudices, and superstitions of those time periods. Some of the writings are historically factual, while others are merely symbolic, to emphasize a particular idea. You cannot read a symbolic or allegorical story and accept it literally. Yet this does not make these stories any less important. In fact, many allegories have much deeper spiritual significance than the literally true and historically factual accounts. But they must be properly interpreted."

"Wow! Where do you find someone who can interpret those stories for you?"

"Good question, Eric! And that illustrates why we have so many different religions in the world. You can compare six or seven traditional Christian sects. . . . They all use the same Bible, and they still have differences of opinion about doctrine. That is an example of the problem of interpretation."

I then asked, "Whose interpretation do *you* use?"

Shimahn chuckled, "I like to believe that I'm using God's interpretation."

At that point in our conversation, Shimahn began paging through a little book that was lying on the table in front of him. The book was bound in black leather and, obviously, had been used extensively, because its edges were very ragged and worn, and the pages were yellow and wrinkled.

I walked up to the table and asked, "Is that a Bible?"

Shimahn frowned as he quickly glanced at Nehemiah. By that time, I had almost forgotten that Nehemiah was in the room. As their eyes met, their mutual smiles revealed that they shared some special secret about the little book.

"You might call it a Bible," Shimahn replied, "but it's quite different from the Bible you're accustomed to reading."

I moved closer to the book and realized that it was written in a foreign language.

"What language is that?" I asked.

"It is an ancient Indian and Tibetan tongue known as 'Vedic Sanskrit.'"

"Why is it written in Sanskrit? Is that language still used?"

"Sanskrit is really not a conversational language," Shimahn said. "Rather, it is an ancient form of expression that was used in the early written works of the first Himalayan masters. We can assume that this is how the revelator of this book heard the Voice of God."

"Does God speak Sanskrit?" I asked.

Again Shimahn chuckled under his breath, but as always in a way that didn't allow me to feel foolish for asking questions.

"Eric, are you familiar with Joan of Arc, the young French girl who was a medieval Christian martyr?"

"I've heard her name."

"Well, she was once asked, 'Does God speak to you in French?' Her reply was, 'I don't know what language God *speaks* in, but I *hear* Him in French.'"

Shimahn certainly had a way of making a point. He always used examples that were easily understandable, even for a beginning student of spiritual wisdom. And as he spoke, his dark eyes were constantly scrutinizing me, penetrating the very depths of my soul. I tried to guess his age as we talked. His olive-colored skin didn't have a wrinkle, his hair was jet black with just a touch of gray at the temples, and his voice was resonant and smooth. My first estimate of Shimahn's age was late thirties, but I wondered how someone so young could have acquired so much knowledge and could speak with such absolute conviction about deep philosophical matters.

While I was savoring Shimahn's last remark about Joan of Arc, I happened to glance over my right shoulder toward the open window that I had peeked through earlier in the day. To my sudden horror, I realized that daylight was gone, and it was dark as coal outside. I had become so engrossed with my two new friends that I had lost all thought about the outside world and my parents. . . . My parents??? Oh, God! My mother will be worried sick about me.

When I had wandered down that side road to where Nehemiah was sitting, I had forgotten that my parents were some distance ahead of me, following a tour guide who was about to take us to Gethsemane and the Mount of Olives. It must have been five or six hours since I had disappeared from them.

Chapter Two

For the first time since we had been together, Shimahn and Nehemiah realized that my family had no idea where I was. And as the two men reacted with alarm, I was overcome by sudden feelings of guilt and remorse. What had I done to the two people I loved most in the world? How could I have been so inconsiderate? I wondered if my parents had continued their tour, possibly assuming that I was in the other bus, or if they still were wandering around the darkened streets of the old city frantically searching for me. Fortunately, my mind was quickly put at ease. A telephone was available just a few doors away from Shimahn's room, and our call got through immediately. We learned that, after unsuccessfully looking around for me on the Via Dolorosa, Mom and Dad finally had given up their search and, reluctantly, had returned to our King David Hotel suite, hoping that, being there, they would receive some word on my whereabouts. After assuring my parents that I was safe, my two spiritually illumined friends agreed that Nehemiah would help me get back to my hotel in the newer section of Jerusalem.

Despite the fact that we were able to hire a taxi quite easily, the old Hebrew was rather silent during the first part of the ride. But even though he seemed to want to sit quietly in deep contemplation, I was determined to question him about Shimahn and about the things I had seen and heard that day.

I broke the silence by asking, "What's inside the little book that Shimahn had on the table?"

Nehemiah paused for a moment and responded, "Absolute Truth, as revealed by the world's great spiritual teachers."

"What do you mean by absolute Truth?" I asked.

Again, he paused before answering. "Pure Truth is very simple," he declared, "but to materialistic human thought, Truth may seem quite radical."

Nehemiah seemed to be struggling to find the proper words. After another brief moment he said:

"When Moses stood before the burning bush on Mt. Horeb, a very basic, yet profound, Truth about the nature of his being was revealed to him; but this Truth would have been so misunderstood by most people of his time that he did not disclose it to them. Instead, he placed a veil over the message and gave the people 'the law'—a series of rules-for-living that they could understand and practice."

Nehemiah looked into my eyes to see if I was following him. I nodded my head to acknowledge that I was. He continued:

"Similarly, while much of what appears in your Bible has a deep hidden meaning, the scriptural material also has been veiled somewhat and presented in a form that the masses can understand and accept. As Shimahn explained to you this afternoon, the essence of the message is all there, but in order to find it, you must sort through a good deal of allegorical symbolism."

I then asked, "What makes Shimahn's little book so different?"

Nehemiah answered, "Most of the allegories and symbolic stories have been omitted. What remains is a purely spiritual record of creation and the unveiled truth of Being, as revealed by Moses, Christ Jesus, and other enlightened masters."

"Wow! Have you read the book?"

"No! I don't understand Sanskrit."

"You mean to say it's never been translated?"

"It may have been, but I have never seen it in any other language."

"What's the name of the book?"

Again he paused for a moment. . . . "In English, I believe it would be translated as 'THE GOSPEL According to I AM'."

I didn't answer, but tried to comprehend what I had just heard. As we arrived at the hotel, I again broke the silence.

"Nehemiah, may I ask you one more question?"

"Of course, Eric!"

"How old is Shimahn?"

He smiled meekly. "We do not like to discuss human age because it is of no significance."

"But do you know how old he is?"

"Well, Eric, I am not absolutely certain—and please do not repeat this—but I have been told that he has passed his eighty-fifth year."

My eyes opened wide as I gasped: "That's impossible! He looks about thirty-five or forty."

"He is not as other men, Eric. He attained Mastership a long time ago and more than likely had reached high levels of spiritual awareness in previous lifetimes."

I didn't even hear Nehemiah's last words as I blurted out, "Then how old are you . . . two-hundred-and-fifty?"

At that, Nehemiah burst into loud laughter. "Oh, Eric, I am sorry to disappoint you, but I will be eighty-eight on my next birthday."

"But that makes you about the same age as Shimahn. How come you look so much older?"

"I did not discover the Mystical Truth Teachings until I was seventy-seven years old, and by that time, the calendar already had taken its toll on my body. . . . But take heart," he smiled, "I don't feel as old as I look."

After that statement, Nehemiah patted the top of my head, and we stepped from the taxi as he paid the driver.

When we arrived at my family's suite, tears of joy were streaming down my mother's face as she embraced me.

"Oh, Eric!" she cried, "we were so worried!"

Meanwhile, Nehemiah was talking to my father, claiming full responsibility for my absence. The old man explained that he and I had met on the street and had become so engrossed in our discussion that we completely lost track of time. He never mentioned Shimahn.

My parents accepted his story, and they exchanged pleasantries as Nehemiah left. After apologizing for putting them through so much trauma, I excused myself and retired to my room.

It now was less than eight hours since I had wandered off that main street in Old Jerusalem, but during that brief period, I had been introduced to more new concepts than some people are exposed to in a lifetime. I don't recall how long I lay there, but eventually I drifted into a calm and restful sleep.

The next morning, I awoke at the first light of dawn. Since my parents probably would not be out of bed for another hour, I lay awake trying to recall some of what I had heard the previous day. My mind was flooded with questions. Was Shimahn really in his eighties. . . ? What was this mysterious spiritual Truth that he spoke about. . . ? Since he was from Tibet, I would have expected him to be a follower of Buddhism, Hinduism, or some other Eastern philosophy. Yet he made many references to Jesus and seemed completely familiar with the Bible. . . . And what about that little book. . . ? What great secrets might be locked in its pages? Something was stirring inside of me, evoking a deep desire to see Shimahn again.

At breakfast my father reminded us that, for the next two days, he would be attending a few business meetings and would be leaving my mother and me on our own. Mother wanted to spend this free time shopping and asked if I would join her. I told her that I really preferred to stay around the hotel, resting and relaxing. She accepted that story and agreed to let me stay, as long as I promised not to go wandering off with any more strange people.

I could make that promise without feeling like a liar, because I no longer considered Shimahn and Nehemiah as strangers but rather as very close friends.

After my parents had gone their separate ways, I looked through our tour books and maps so I could become better acquainted with the city of Jerusalem. I wanted to determine the best way to get back to the area around Golgotha. With a little bit of ingenuity, I was able to plot a public bus route to my destination, an approach that was far less expensive than hiring a taxi. Even though I had brought a fair amount of spending money with me, I still had to watch my budget.

After arriving at a familiar-looking location in Old Jerusalem, I exited from the bus and walked to the area near Saint Stephen's Gate and the Via Dolorosa. From there, I followed my path of the previous day to the point where I had first met Nehemiah. I then proceeded around the next corner to the building where I was introduced to Shimahn. Again the door was closed tightly, but this time the lower window also was closed and was covered by a curtain which prevented me from seeing inside the room.

Somewhat dejected, I slid down to the concrete step, pondering my next move. After a few minutes, five people, all dressed in western-hemisphere casual attire, approached the building and knocked on the door. Almost instantaneously, a woman wearing a Moslem veil opened the door and offered them entry. I jumped to my feet and followed them down the steps, acting as if I were one of their group.

At the bottom of the stairs, Nehemiah was standing in the doorway, personally welcoming each of the guests into the room. As he was shaking hands with the man directly in front of me, he glanced over the man's shoulder and noticed my presence for the first time. Smiling demurely as he shook his head from side-to-side, the old Hebrew firmly placed his hand on my shoulder and escorted me to a room across the hall.

"What are you doing here, Eric?" he asked. "Do your parents know where you are?"

I answered, "They're busy today, and they told me that I could entertain myself in any way that would keep me out of trouble. I certainly won't find any trouble here, will I?" Nehemiah frowned quizzically, and then I said, "I want to spend more time with you and Shimahn. . . . I want to learn more about Truth."

He replied, "As I told you yesterday, Eric, Shimahn is very busy at this time. He's going to begin teaching these people in about a half hour."

"But you told me that he wouldn't be speaking again until next Tuesday in Cairo!"

"That is his next public lecture. Before that time he'll be conducting a series of private classes for his more advanced, serious students."

"But I would like to be a serious student. . . . Couldn't I attend these classes?"

He stammered momentarily: "Well . . . ah . . . in the first place, most of his classes here are being given in Hebrew."

"But the people who came in ahead of me looked like Americans."

"Yes! Well, today will be one of his few classes presented in English."

"Then I should be able to listen in."

"I don't know, Eric, that could pose a problem. . . ."

"Please, Nehemiah!"

"All right, I'll see what I can do. You wait here while I discuss this with Shimahn. But remember now . . . I am not promising anything."

He then left me alone in the room and went through a doorway at the end of the hall. As I looked around the room, I was overcome by an eerie feeling of deja vu. I felt as if I had been there before. The floor was concrete, and the walls were constructed of the drab limestone that abounds in the area.

Standing to one side of the room was a very, very old table. The table was long and narrow and could easily have seated a dozen people. Looking at the table in front of the limestone wall, I began to visualize this as the setting for Jesus and his Disciples at the Last Supper. While my mind was conjuring up this sacred scene, Nehemiah re-entered the room and broke the spell.

"All right, Eric," he said, "Shimahn will allow you to attend the morning session. But first, let me outline a few rules and procedures.

"This is a lecture, not a public discussion; so you will not be allowed to ask any questions. Also, when you enter the room you will notice that most of the students will be sitting with their eyes closed. Please honor this silence by joining them in meditation. In these class sessions, we try to prepare ourselves for a mystical experience. The words spoken by the teacher are important, but they only constitute the 'Letter of Truth.' Our goal is to become imbued with the 'Spirit of Truth'—to feel the very Presence of God that resides within our own being. The spoken words are stepping-stones which prepare our consciousness for this experience. . . . But the experience of Christ-consciousness is our real reason for being here."

Nehemiah looked into my eyes, and I nodded my head in agreement. Then, after a brief pause, he escorted me to the meeting room where eleven people were sitting in silence with their eyes closed. I quietly took a seat in the last row and tried to follow Nehemiah's instructions.

Within a few minutes, Shimahn entered the room and sat at a small wooden table. He bowed his head in salutation as he slowly glanced around the room. Then he folded his hands on the table in front of him and closed his eyes.

I also closed my eyes and tried to ponder some of the new concepts that had recently been presented to me. While I could feel the obvious peace in the room, I can't say that I had any transcendental or mystical experience during the meditation.

After about fifteen minutes, Shimahn began to speak:

"Good morning, Friends! Today, we will begin by discussing the true nature of God. . . ."

And with that, he reiterated many of the points he had made in our conversation on the previous day. Once again he stressed the infinite allness of God and the fact that nothing exists outside of God's Own Being.

"God *IS!*" he said, "and that is all we need to know. God is Infinite Consciousness . . . and that Divine Consciousness is eternally revealing and disclosing Itself ... *as* Itself . . . *to* Itself. The specific event that theologians usually refer to as 'creation' was not just a one-time phenomenon but actually is an ongoing process of Infinite Consciousness unfolding Itself *as* the spiritual universe. This activity of Consciousness unfolding is really God appearing in an individual way *as* you and *as* me. . . . Immortal, Eternal Life expressing Itself as your life and mine. All that God Is, I Am. . . . My body is the holy temple of God. Your body is the temple of God. But remember, in speaking of body, we are not referring to this three-dimensional, physical-concept-of-body that is our normal point of reference.

"The first chapter of Genesis states that man has been created in the image and likeness of God. This is a Cause-and-effect relationship. But in order for us to properly understand the effect (man), we must gain some comprehension of the nature of the Cause (God).

"God is Infinite Spirit. . . . Therefore, His image and likeness must be spiritual. God is Eternal Life. . . . Therefore, you and I are that very same Life expressed in a distinctly individual form. God is Infinite Consciousness.... Therefore, we are the specific activity of Consciousness unfolding."

At that point Shimahn stopped speaking and closed his eyes to give each of us a moment to digest what had just been said. After that brief period, he continued: "God-Consciousness is expressing and revealing Itself as the uniquely individual consciousness that I am. . . . My body, which is spiritual, is really the incorporeal embodiment of all of God's attributes. . . . The place whereon I stand is Holy Ground, because 'I and my Father are One'. . . ."

Again Shimahn became silent and closed his eyes. During that silent period, I realized that this master from the Himalayas had just clarified one of my childhood dilemmas. When I first learned in Sunday school that I was created in the image and likeness of God, I reasoned backward from effect to Cause. I looked at my finite, material body and projected that vision up to the divine. I was creating for myself a very humanistic concept of Deity. But today Shimahn had given me a whole new perspective on this matter. He instructed us to begin our reasoning with a recognition of God as infinite, incorporeal Spirit. From that standpoint, the logical conclusion is: if God is Spirit, then the image and likeness of God must be of the same substance. In other words, my real identity and my true body are spiritual—not material.

Shimahn again began to speak: "A moment ago, I stated that your body is the 'Temple of God' and that this Temple is spiritual in nature. Then what about this three-dimensional, physical form that we think of as 'me'?

"There is not a spiritual universe *and* a material universe. There is not a spiritual body *and* a material body. There is only one universe and it is spiritual. You have only one body and it is spiritual. But the spiritual realm cannot be perceived by our five physical senses. The spiritual universe is of a fourth dimension and can be discerned only by a transcendental, fourth-dimensional state of consciousness. We cannot see God, or our own true identity, with three-dimensional vision.

"Consequently, this form that we acknowledge as a physical body living in a material universe is merely a false concept of our body and the universe. As Paul said: 'For now we see through a glass, darkly; but then face to face: now I know in part; but then shall I know even as also I am known.' Elucidating the same theme, Christ Jesus told us to judge not by appearances but to 'judge righteous judgement.'

And later, in the first Epistle of John, we read: 'Beloved, now are we the sons of God, and it doth not yet appear what we shall be: but we know that, when He shall appear, we shall be like Him; for we shall see Him as He is.'

"These quotations are examples of the spiritual thread that is woven throughout the scriptures of the world. Many people completely overlook these passages, or else they interpret them as having application only in some future after-life. But when these statements are read with spiritual discernment, they corroborate the points I have just made about our limited concept of reality."

Glancing around the room with his penetrating dark eyes, Shimahn paused for a moment. . . . Then he continued: "Now that we realize that we have been functioning under an illusory, false sense of existence, we may ask the questions: 'How do I become aware of ultimate reality? How do I develop that transcendental consciousness in which I can "see" myself as I really Am?' The answer is: through prayer and meditation—or, as Brother Lawrence, the seventeenth century mystic, once described it, through 'The Practice of the Presence of God.'

"To 'practice the Presence' is to make a specific effort of becoming aware of the Presence of God within us. In the early stages of our spiritual development, we must consciously fill our mind with thoughts of truth.

"In our common, everyday human mental activity, we entertain thoughts that reflect our personal desires, concerns and fears. Our spare time is often occupied by daydreams which, like our sleeping night dreams, have been influenced by our heredity, environment, and personal human history. These daydreams or mental meanderings are of no real benefit and actually keep us enmeshed in a very materialistic state of consciousness.

"But after our introduction to spiritual wisdom, we begin to exercise some degree of control over our mind's activities. While at first this may seem like nothing more than mental gymnastics, what we are doing is filling our mind with thoughts of truth. This, in turn, is preparing our consciousness to become receptive to the 'Word of God.'

"To most religious people, prayer is an activity in which they petition God for those things or circumstances that they desire. First they give God a list of their personal requirements—as if the infinite, all-knowing Consciousness needed to be informed by them. Then they ask, plead with, or even beg God to answer their specific requests. In most cases, these unillumined people actually expect the omniscient Divine Principle of this universe to bestow upon them whatever favors they have asked for. What a childish, humanistic approach to Deity!

"A God of Spirit is aware of nothing but Its Own infinite Self-containment. God knows only spiritual verities and is not even conscious of our materialistic, false concept of existence. To ask God to function in the human realm would be like asking the equation 'two times two equals four' to do something when we multiply 'two times two' and get 'five'. What does four know about five? What can four do about the false sense of five? What can a God Who is Spirit do about our erroneous, illusory belief of materiality?

"Jesus said: 'God is. . .Spirit: and they that worship Him must worship Him in spirit and in truth.' The Master told us not to pray for the things of this world. Instead, he commanded us to 'Seek ye first the kingdom of God, and His righteousness,' and then he followed that statement with the promise that 'all these things shall be added unto you.' When he was asked about the kingdom of God, he replied: 'My kingdom is not of this world.' And when he was further questioned on where to find this kingdom, he declared: 'Neither shall they say, Lo here! or, lo there! for, behold, the kingdom of God is within you!'

"How could he have said it more clearly? We are not to pray for things! We are not to ask God to fulfill our human desires!

"Then, what is true prayer. . . ?

"By instructing us to seek the kingdom of God that is within us, the Master is directing us to turn to the spiritual center of our own being. . . . And I must tell you, from my personal experience, that this is not easy to do while your mind is filled with thoughts of 'this world.'

"Each of us must find time—hopefully several times a day—when we can get away from the crowd and 'come out from among them and be. . .separate.' We must allot ourselves specific periods that are devoted exclusively to practicing the Presence of God—to consciously knowing this truth that we have learned.

"But let me stress right here and now that simply thinking thoughts about Truth is also not true prayer. Making parrot-like statements to yourself is really no different than repeating affirmations or formulas, and this is a procedure that many students of metaphysical religions already have discovered is of very little value.

"Certainly, a mind filled with thoughts of spiritual Truth is more desirable than a mind immersed in the fears, doubts, and desires of gross materialism. But please remember this: Any thoughts about Truth are not Truth Itself but merely thoughts *about* Truth. Any words about God, whether spoken on a lecture platform or written in a book, are just that: words *about* God.

"When we transcend the thinking processes and reach a point beyond the activity of the human mind, we become a state of receptivity that is capable of hearing the 'Word of God.' Then we no longer have just words *about* God but, rather, the 'Word' which *Is* God. At that mystical moment, we no longer have mere thoughts about Truth, but rather Truth Itself uttering Its voice. That, then, is true prayer . . . not my talking to God or making statements about God, but the very Spirit of God announcing Itself within me."

Once again, Shimahn paused for a moment. . . . Then he concluded this class session by saying: "Now let us have a period of silent meditation. . . . Close your eyes and allow your mind to become still. . . . Try to feel that Presence of God within you. . . . If you are unable to achieve the silence—if your mind continues to think worldly thoughts—then begin with a period of contemplative meditation. Silently reflect upon a statement about the truth that we have discussed today. Possibly a scriptural passage will come to you. Whatever your individual approach, remember that your goal is to reach a point beyond the thinking process where you become totally quiet and receptive to the 'Word of God'. . . ."

Shimahn then stopped speaking and a great silence and peace permeated the room. It was during this meditation that I had my first mystical experience. And from that day forward, my life would never be the same. . . .

Chapter Three

How do you tell someone about your first mystical experience? How do you describe the sensation? The best answer is: Don't!

It has been suggested that if you speak about spiritual wisdom before it has taken root and truly is a part of your consciousness, you run the risk of losing what you have. This can be compared to planting seeds in the soil of your garden and then, instead of fertilizing and watering the plants and giving them time to grow, you dig up the soil every few days to show the world your beautiful seeds. In the first stages of our spiritual studies, we are given seeds of truth. These seeds, planted in the garden of our consciousness, must be cultivated, nurtured, and given an opportunity to take root.

As a reader of this book, you may ask the question: How do you know when you have had a mystical- or God-experience? In pondering this question, I am reminded of a television talk show that I was watching some time ago. A psychologist, who was an expert in the field of marital relationships, was asked: "How do you know when you're in love?" Her answer was: "If you have to ask . . . You're not!"

How do I know that I had a mystical experience in Shimahn's class in Old Jerusalem. . . ? I just *know!*

At the conclusion of the meditation period, Shimahn said, "Thank you!" as he quietly stepped from behind the speaker's table and left the meeting room. Some of the students continued to sit in silence, trying to prolong whatever it was they personally were experiencing. Others rose from their chairs and departed from the room without speaking. I, too, felt a quietness and serenity that produced a mood in which I didn't want to converse with anyone. All of us were islands unto ourselves, savoring that indescribable moment when we had seen God "face to face."

Eventually I stepped out of the room and while doing that I met Nehemiah in the hallway. He caught my eye and silently gestured toward the room across the hall where we had had our earlier conversation. After we entered the room, he closed the door and motioned for me to sit at the old long table. For a brief interval we shared a moment of peace, looking at each other without exchanging any words.

Then, finally, I said, "Oh, Nehemiah, it was a wonderful experience!"

He smiled and said, "I am pleased that you had an opportunity to be with us today, Eric. It was a most receptive group, and we were able to achieve a superb level of awareness."

"Will Shimahn be speaking again today?" I asked.

"Yes, he will . . . later on this afternoon."

"May I attend that class?"

Shaking his head from side to side, he said, "I sincerely feel that you have received an abundance of spiritual manna today, Eric. You have been given the seeds of absolute Truth. . . . Now it is up to you to take these seeds and nurture them within yourself so they can take root and grow. Work with these principles. Allow them to become a part of your consciousness, and they will bear fruit richly. The mystical experience that you had this morning is your first step on the path to enlightenment. A spark has been ignited at the center of your soul and, ultimately, it will lead you to your own spiritual fulfillment."

I blinked my eyes in agreement as Nehemiah continued: "For these reasons I do not feel it is advisable for you to stay for this afternoon's class. And in addition to all of that—being practical and coming down to the level of 'this world'—we don't want your parents to find you missing again, do we?"

Reluctantly, I had to admit that he was right. There probably would be just enough time for me to return to the hotel without alarming my mother again. But I had a few more questions that needed answering.

"Nehemiah, I just don't know how I'll remember all the things Shimahn told us today."

"Do not worry about that, Eric. Most people will not recall all the words. But as Shimahn stressed in his lecture, the words spoken by the teacher are just words. . . . They have no power of themselves. They are only foundational stepping-stones that guide us on the path to enlightenment. However, if you make a practice of turning within to the spiritual center of your own being, you will continue to be taught. But what you learn there will be absolute Truth, because you will be hearing the 'Word of God.' Please remember that your real Teacher is within you and, therefore, will always. be with you."

"Gosh! I sure hope you're right, Nehemiah."

Then he stood up and said, "Well, Eric, I suggest we get you back on a bus so your parents will know that they still have a son."

"All right, Nehemiah, you win! I'll be getting out of your hair for today."

Rising from my chair, I looked at my dear old friend with tears in my eyes and then threw myself into his arms as I gave him a huge bearhug. After that poignant moment, he put his hand on my shoulder and escorted me through the door and up the steps. By the time we stepped out into the mid-day sunlight, the tears which had been welling up in my eyes were now rolling down my face. Without another word, I began trotting away from him along the old cobblestone street. After a few strides, I glanced back over my shoulder. Nehemiah was still standing in the doorway, waving to me. I spun around without breaking stride, waved once, and continued on around the corner. After a few more steps, I stopped jogging and walked the rest of the way to my bus stop.

I recall nothing of the ride back to the hotel. While spiritually this should have been a very exciting time for me, I was letting human emotions and personal relationships govern my outlook. I do remember exiting from the bus and walking through the hotel lobby. Coincidentally, my mother had just returned from shopping and was at the front desk, inquiring if we had any messages.

"Hi, Mom!" I said.

"Oh, Eric, there you are! I was just going to come up to the room to meet you. Your dad should be back soon and we'll probably have an early dinner. Okay?"

"Sure, Mom. Anything you say."

Then I went up to our suite and spent a relaxing half hour soaking in the bathtub.

After a quiet dinner together and a short stroll in the vicinity of our hotel, my parents and I retired early. As I lay in bed, I tried to meditate, applying some of the procedures Shimahn had given us in the class. But apparently the emotional strain of the day had taken its toll, and I quickly fell asleep.

The next day was to be our last full day in Jerusalem. At breakfast, my father rehearsed the speech he'd be giving later that morning, and my mother outlined her plans to investigate one more shopping area near the hotel. I had only one silent desire: that was to be with Shimahn and Nehemiah one last time. After all, I never did thank Shimahn for his wonderful teaching, nor did I even say goodbye to him.

As soon as my parents had left for their respective destinations, I once again boarded my bus to Old Jerusalem. During the ride, I noticed that the sky was extremely overcast. This was the first ominously dreary day since we had arrived in Israel.

Upon leaving the bus, I again walked the path that, by that time, was becoming as familiar to me as the alley behind my parents' home in suburban Chicago. I arrived at the old limestone building, and as usual the door was closed tightly. On that overcast morning, however, the curtains on the basement window were parted, so I could easily see into the room. The chairs, which had been neatly arranged for the previous day's classwork, were gone and the room looked very stark and barren. For a fleeting moment, I felt a sense of panic as the thought came that maybe they had left that location and were no longer conducting classes there.

I slumped down to the concrete step and sat quietly for awhile, hoping that someone would approach the building. After about fifteen minutes of fruitless waiting, I decided to make my presence known. I stood up and meekly knocked on the door. Getting no response, I knocked a little more forcefully. Within a few seconds, a young woman, who apparently was a native of the area, opened the door.

She looked at me inquisitively as I asked, "Is Shimahn here today?" She didn't respond but looked even more puzzled. "Is Nehemiah here?" She still gave no reply. In a louder voice I asked, "Do you know Shimahn. . . ? Is he here?"

Haltingly, in very broken English, she replied, "Shimahn . . . he go Egypt."

"No!" I shouted. "You can't mean that! Is Nehemiah here?"

"He go Egypt, too," she said, as she smiled apologetically. Then she shrugged her shoulders and closed the door.

I leaned against the stone wall as I looked at the people scurrying by in the street. My head began to spin, and for a moment I thought I might faint. But instead, I sat down again on the step, allowing my mind to become inundated by many frustrating questions:

Why didn't Nehemiah tell me yesterday that they were leaving? Was I never to see them again? I wouldn't even know how to contact Shimahn if I ever needed him. Where in Tibet does he live? Does he have an address? Can I write to him? And what about Nehemiah? My wonderful, dear friend Nehemiah. . . . Does he have a last name?

I had assumed he was a native of this area and lived nearby. I was certain that Nehemiah could always contact Shimahn for me. But I didn't even know how to contact Nehemiah.

I rose to my feet and wandered up and down the street in front of the building, looking for a sign of recognition or familiarity from the people passing by. I approached a few of them, but apparently they didn't speak English. When I mentioned Shimahn's name, they just looked at me with a blank stare and walked away.

I stood in the midst of the traffic and thought: "Is this all there is to it? Is this how it all ends? Yesterday, a great spiritual event was taking place in that room down the street, and these people aren't even aware of it . . . nor do they care! Is this how it was for Jesus? He walked up and down some of these same streets, but only a few even came close to understanding his message. Then in the end all his friends deserted him, and he was crucified for what he taught.

"Oh, Shimahn! Why did you have to leave. . . ?"

Chapter Four

I aimlessly wandered around on that street in Old Jerusalem for about an hour. Finally the futility of the situation hit me, and I somberly drifted back to the bus stop where I could get my ride back to the King David Hotel.

At dinner, my parents became aware of my lingering despondency. Since I had given them no indication of what was troubling me, they concluded that I probably was homesick for my friends and personal environment. I didn't say anything to dispel their assumption.

Later that evening as I climbed into bed, my mind was overwhelmed by a sensation of aloneness. What kind of teaching is this if I can't share it with those who are closest to me? Even if I felt compelled to say something about it, how could I begin to repeat what I had heard?

Shimahn had such a command of the language that the words of his message flowed so very naturally. I wondered if he appeared just as eloquent when he taught the people in Hebrew or in some other language . . . other language. . . ? "Gosh," I pondered, "how many languages could he speak?" One thing was certain: he obviously could read Sanskrit.

And what about that little book? Would I ever have an opportunity to study its contents?

After those fruitless deliberations, it occurred to me to meditate. Nehemiah had told me that I could always find peace through meditation. In the class, Shimahn had said that we must allow our mind to become quiet—to stop thinking worldly thoughts. But there was no way that I could stop the clamor in my mind on this particular evening.

In the past, if I had wanted something as badly as I wanted to see my two friends today, I might have said a prayer to God, asking Him to fulfill my wishes. But after all I had learned in the last two days, that now would appear to be an exercise in futility.

"Shimahn! What have you done? You've taken my God away from me!!!"

The next morning, after an early breakfast, my parents and I took the train ride from Jerusalem back to the Tel Aviv airport. Then at 3:30 in the afternoon, we boarded a DC-9 fan jet for the trip to Chicago. Our flight plan routed us westward over the length of the Mediterranean Sea along the North African coastline. As we soared over the Strait of Gibraltar and headed out across the Atlantic Ocean, I had the feeling that, on that particular day, the sun might never set for us. For a brief period, it seemed like our airplane might hold its own in a race with the sun to the western horizon. However, by the time we were two hours out over the Atlantic, the sun had won the race. The sky outside our cabin windows was dark and seemed almost as barren as I was feeling at that time.

After dinner, as the cabin lights were dimmed, I closed my eyes and tried to contemplate some of the spiritual principles I had learned during the past two days. Shimahn had told me that God was the essence and substance of my being. So I tried to turn to the kingdom of God within me, hoping to find some sense of direction there.

Without thinking too many thoughts, I was able to achieve a degree of silence and the peace that followed quite naturally. Though I heard no words and received no specific instructions in my meditation, I did reach a level of awareness that erased my concerns about the future. The realization came that, if I continued to work with these principles, I would always be led to whatever and whoever were necessary for the fulfillment of my purpose in life.

The remainder of our flight was quite restful, and we arrived at Chicago's O'Hare Field ten minutes ahead of schedule.

During the next several weeks, I very quickly fell back into the normal routine of the final days of summer vacation—but with one interesting exception. Every now and then my neighborhood friends and I would become embroiled in one of our "heavy" philosophical discussions. More often than not, these conversations would come to an abrupt halt as I dramatically made some profound statement of spiritual wisdom. The others would look at me in awe, wondering where I had learned such things. I tried not to flaunt this newfound knowledge, but I did enjoy the occasional moments of amazement and quasi-respect. Looking back now, I realize that I was running the risk of having my "pearls trampled under foot."

With the advent of the new school year, I became more engrossed in the activities of "this world." Those exciting two days in Old Jerusalem were quickly fading into the dark recesses of my mind. Were Shimahn and Nehemiah real people or merely figments of my imagination. . . ? Did I actually have a mystical experience that morning in the old limestone building. . . ? Did it really matter?

At that particular time, my outer life was running fairly smoothly. My grades were adequate, and I was a starting guard on my junior-high-school basketball team. There were pep rallies and dances, and I even was able to get a part-time job stocking shelves in a local grocery store.

Because of all this "worldly activity," I very seldom gave any thought to my spiritual adventure in Old Jerusalem, and I had little motivation to practice the principles I had learned there. But the following April, during our Easter recess from school, I was involved in an incident that reawakened my interest in mysticism.

For that holiday period, my parents and I had driven to St. Louis, Missouri, to spend a week with my mother's brother Arthur and his family. This gave me an opportunity to renew my childhood friendship with my cousin Pamela. Pam is ten months younger than I, and we shared some memorable experiences during our early years when her family still lived in the Chicago area.

On the second last day of our visit, Pamela and I were walking through a neighborhood park with three of her close friends: two other girls Pam's age and a boy named Thomas, who was a few years older than the rest of us. We were involved in one of those speculative discussions that so often occupy the leisure time of young people. As we found a warm sunny patch of grass to relax on, one of the girls made a comment about the great wonder of the physical universe.

Kathy said, "When I look at the stars in the sky at night, I am just amazed by what I see." She then asked, "Do any of you believe that the universe is infinite?"

Thomas answered, "I don't! I find it very difficult to believe that there are no boundaries, or that the universe never began and will never end."

Then Diane interjected, "But, Tom, if there was a beginning, what existed before the beginning? And if there is a boundary in space, what is beyond that boundary? Personally, I accept the theory that the universe is infinite."

Pam then said, "Frankly, I haven't thought that much about the 'whys and wherefores' of existence. I only know that I have faith in God, and I believe that the universe and our personal lives are all part of a divine plan."

She then turned toward me and asked, "What do you think, Eric?" as her three friends also looked in my direction.

Before I could answer, a dignified-looking elderly gentleman, who apparently had been listening to us from a nearby park bench, stood up and began walking toward our little group. Short of stature, the man looked as if he, through some unexplainable time warp, had just stepped out of the pre-prohibition era. He was nattily dressed in a three-piece gray, pin-striped suit and had a heavy gold watch chain hanging from his vest pocket. Sitting down on the grass with us and smiling as he looked directly into my eyes, this diminutive stranger then proclaimed: "Eric doesn't think . . . he *knows!*"

I quickly glanced at my friends as their mouths dropped open, and their eyes widened in a state of mini-shock.

"And just who the hell are you?" Tom asked.

"I am Mr. Hunt," the man replied.

Feeling a bit surprised by the mysterious intrusion of this strange little man, I then spoke up: "Excuse me, sir, but do you know Shimahn?"

"Yes!" he answered.

"What's a Shimahn?" Tom interrupted.

"Never mind that for now!" Mr. Hunt retorted. "I believe we were discussing infinity!"

My four friends looked at each other inquisitively as the distinguished-looking gentleman continued: "To a certain degree, each of you is partially correct in your present analysis. The real universe *is* infinite . . . but that universe is also spiritual. The physical-sense-of-universe that you see with your eyes is only a materialistic concept of reality and, therefore, is not infinite."

Not wanting to offend this seemingly well-meaning man, my friends and I quickly glanced at each other and, by silent mutual consent, agreed to humor him for awhile.

Kathy then continued the conversation by asking, "Uh, Mr. Hunt . . . what do you mean by 'physical sense of universe' and 'materialistic concept of reality'?"

"That's a good question, Kathy." He hesitated for a moment and then said, "As you know, most of us, in our early religious training, were taught that God is omnipotent, omnipresent, and omniscient. . . . Yet, for some reason, we have not accepted the full implication of that teaching. Kathy, you asked the initial question about infinity. But do you really understand what that word means?"

She replied, "I believe I do, Mr. Hunt. If something is infinite, it would be unlimited and have no boundaries. I suppose you could assume that the infinite is everywhere and fills all space."

The little man then responded, "That is correct, Kathy. But in addition to its relationship to space, the infinite also has an eternal relationship to time. In other words, infinity never began and will never end. . . . It just *IS!*"

As the conversation progressed, it seemed that my friends were becoming quite intrigued by this message of truth. They all began participating in the dialogue, and several of them appeared to be responding quite positively to the ideas that were being presented.

Pamela then spoke up: "Mr. Hunt, that concept of eternity has always been a problem for me. When Eric and I first started going to Sunday school, we were told that 'God always was and always will be.' But I just can't comprehend the idea of 'no beginning.'"

"I'm glad you brought that up, Pam," he replied. "It is very natural to look at the physical universe and, because of our limited sense-perception, assume that everything is material and, therefore, was created or had a beginning. But God is not a physical being. . . . God is Immortal Spirit—the One Universal Life, whose existence never began and will never end."

Mr. Hunt glanced at each of us, who by that time were all listening very intently.

"Let me give you an example," he said. "We all agree that two-times-two equals four. Now I ask you the questions: When did two-times-two become four. . . ? Was there ever a time in the past when two-times-two did not equal four. . . ? Will there ever be a time in the future when two-times-two will cease being four?"

In response to each of these questions, my friends and I gestured in agreement as Mr. Hunt continued. "We all must learn to recognize God—not as some kind of super-human being—but rather as the incorporeal, Divine Principle of the universe. Think of words like 'truth' and 'law', and then you'll begin to understand the eternal nature of God."

As he finished that sentence, I realized that this uninvited stranger had just clarified another of my childhood dilemmas. I now could more easily comprehend and accept the fundamental truth that God exists "from everlasting—to everlasting." I also realized that if this is true of God, then it must be just as true of me, since I am the perfect and complete expression of God's Being.

At that point, Mr. Hunt looked directly into my eyes and said: "If each of us can accept the infinite allness of God, we then can follow with certain logical deductions. As you all know, the first chapter of Genesis states that man has been created in the image and likeness of God. What would the image and likeness of infinite Spirit be like?"

No one answered, so he continued: "God is eternal Life. God is infinite Consciousness, the only Intelligence, the one all-inclusive Substance. Therefore, this outer world, which we perceive as a physical universe peopled with mortal beings, is nothing more than an illusion—our false sense of the divine reality. And that illusory state is a mere counterfeit of the true spiritual universe, which continues to unfold as the Godhead expresses Itself in an infinite variety of forms. The only activity that really is going on, then, can be described as 'Divine Consciousness unfolding Itself.'"

Again, Mr. Hunt paused briefly and glanced at each of us.

Thomas took that opportunity to speak up: "What makes you such an authority on all this? Are you a priest, or a minister?"

"No, Tom! I have no human ordination. Like most of you, I am merely a humble seeker after Truth."

"What is Truth?" Tom asked pensively.

Mr. Hunt smiled as he recognized the historical irony of that question. He then said, "God is Truth! Therefore, I am constantly seeking a more complete knowledge of God. Long ago I realized that, as I attain an understanding of the true nature of God, I will receive the answers to all my questions about life and about my very own existence. Jesus once declared: 'And this is life eternal, that they might know Thee the only true God, and Jesus Christ, whom Thou hast sent.' In that statement, the Master is telling us that to know God aright is our key to eternal life."

My cousin Pamela interrupted. "Mr. Hunt, do you really think it's possible to understand the nature of God? Or, as you put it, 'to know God aright'?"

"Yes I do, Pam," he responded, "but I don't claim that this is an easy task. 'To know God aright' can be the work of many lifetimes. You see, each of us has a divine, or spiritual, nature which is the real essence and substance of what we are. But this spiritual nature cannot be perceived by our five physcial senses. When we look at our body, we are merely seeing a physical concept of that body. Our real body—our individual divine identity—is the image and likeness of God and, therefore, that identity is spiritual. Tell me, can any of you actually believe that your physical body is the image and likeness of God?"

No one answered audibly, but the three girls shook their heads in unison, as a collective negative response.

"Of course not!" the little man declared.

Kathy then asked, "Mr. Hunt, does that mean that we have two bodies: one that is spiritual, and one that is material?"

"No, Kathy!" he replied.

"But then, if our physical body is not real, wouldn't a person die if he eliminated his body?"

"That's a good question, Kathy . . . but now please remember, you don't have two bodies. You have only one body, and it is spiritual. The problem for most of us is that, as the Apostle Paul told us, we are seeing our body and our universe 'through a glass darkly.' So to answer your question, Kathy, you won't die, because you won't be eliminating or getting rid of your body. All that you will be discarding is your false concept of your body. When you perceive your true spiritual identity, you will be 'putting off the old man'—the 'natural man,' as Paul called it—and you will be seeing yourself as the perfect child of God, which is your real identity. . . . And this body, this identity, will never die. It is birthless and deathless. It is the immortal Melchizedek."

After that statement, there was a brief period of silence as we all contemplated the remarkable truth that had just been presented to us. While the words had a fairly familiar ring for me, and I felt a deep inner agreement with the message, my mind was churning with many new questions:

Just who is Mr. Hunt? What is his relationship to Shimahn? Is he one of Shimahn's students? Perchance was he present at the classwork in Old Jerusalem? Otherwise how could he possibly have known me? And what about Shimahn's little book, "The Gospel According to 'I AM'". . . ? Might Mr. Hunt have a copy?

As I was pondering these questions, our friend Thomas suddenly stood up and said, "Well, that's an interesting story, but I think I've heard enough. Are any of you coming with me?"

Kathy responded, "Tom, don't you think it's a bit rude to expect us to just walk away like that. After all, Mr. Hunt has given us a good deal of time here, and I think the ideas he has presented are quite fascinating."

"Come on, Kathy! You certainly don't believe all that stuff, do you?" Tom retorted.

Then Pam said: "Oh, Thomas, why don't you just leave! You're the most argumentative person I've ever known. You never seem to agree with anything. Today is Friday, but you probably don't believe that tomorrow will be Saturday. I suspect that you even doubt that your name is Thomas!"

Mr. Hunt laughed openly at Pamela's last sentence as Tom asked, "Well, is anyone coming?"

Then Diane, the third girl in our group, rose to her feet and said, "Sure, Tom, I think I'd better head for home, too."

Thomas smiled proudly as Diane joined him. Realizing that the rest of us were not ready to leave, the two of them turned away and began walking down the pathway that my friends and I had followed when we entered the park.

Returning his attention to the three of us who remained, the neatly tailored little man asked if we wanted to continue our discussion. The two girls nodded enthusiastically. They both appeared to be most receptive to his message.

After a momentary pause, Kathy immediately brought us back to the subject: "Mr. Hunt, the things you've been telling us certainly make a lot of sense. But why aren't these ideas known to the whole world?"

He replied: "I am pleased to hear that you recognize the obvious logic in all this, Kathy. Now to answer your question: These ideas have been known for thousands of years. But these principles have been fully understood only by a relatively small number of highly enlightened souls. Portions of this great Truth can be found in the 'Upanishads' and in the 'Bhagavad-gita', the ancient writings which provided much of the foundational material for the Buddhist and Hindu religions. Similarly, many of these same principles are presented in the early Hebrew scriptures and in the books of 'Holy Writ' that have been compiled as the Christian Bible. But while these fundamental laws about the nature of reality have been included in the various sacred writings, in most cases the real message has been veiled and can be discerned only by those whose consciousness has undergone a degree of spiritual illumination. In other words, those people who are living exclusively at a materialistic level of life—those who never have had a 'God experience'—are virtually incapable of recognizing the hidden truth that exists within the Holy Scriptures of the world."

Pamela then asked, "Mr. Hunt, what do you mean by a 'God experience'?"

"Good question, Pam!" he responded. "If we are living a life that is only aware of the activities of 'this world'—a life that relies solely on the testimony of the five physical senses—we can never know God aright. Jesus said, 'My kingdom is not of this world,' and then he told us that that kingdom is to be found within our own being. God is Spirit and does not function in 'this world.' God, the Divine Principle of the spiritual universe, has no knowledge of a suppositional, three-dimensional physical realm. So in order for us to bring ourselves under the law of God—to become aware of the omnipresence of God—we must direct our attention away from the outer world of appearances and turn to that divine kingdom that the Master promised is within each of us. When we succeed in this activity, we achieve the 'God experience'."

Kathy interrupted, "Does this have anything to do with meditation?"

"Yes!" he replied. "But the word 'meditation' carries a number of different connotations."

Pam then said, "When I think of meditation, I visualize a statue of Buddha . . . or I see a person sitting in a cross-legged yoga position."

"You're right, Pam," Mr. Hunt responded. "That is often the image that comes to mind when people think of that word. But true meditation is not exclusively an Oriental practice. Jesus spent a great deal of time in meditation, as did most of the other notable Christian mystics."

I then spoke up. "Mr. Hunt, you just called Jesus a 'mystic'. That's the second time I've heard someone refer to him in that way. Doesn't the word 'mystic' often imply something slightly spooky, or occult?"

"Yes, Eric!" he replied. "In the past, some uninformed people have classified mysticism with spiritualism and other occult philosophies. But today, mysticism is properly understood as 'direct communion with ultimate reality.' In other words, a mystic is someone who communicates with God or receives a direct impartation from God."

"Wow! That must be an exciting experience," Pamela said.

"It certainly can be, Pam," he replied. "But most of the time our meditations merely reach a point of absolute silence, where we have gone beyond the activity of the thinking mind. In that state of peaceful receptivity, we may receive a message, or we may not. However, we should never begin our meditation with a desire to achieve some effect. We must be satisfied just to reach that point of receptive silence. Then if our consciousness is grounded in spiritual Truth, there will be fruitage in our life."

The girls' enthusiasm became even more apparent as Kathy then asked, "Mr, Hunt, could you teach us how to meditate?"

"Well, Kathy, we certainly can discuss the first steps in meditation. As you know, if you wish to develop any specialized skill, you must practice that skill. It takes practice to play the violin, to hit a baseball, or to speak a foreign language. So you also will have to practice if you want to develop the art of meditation."

He continued: "Let's try meditating for a few moments right now. Just sit comfortably and close your eyes. Shutting out the distractions of 'this world' helps to quiet the mind and makes us more receptive to the inner stillness. The next step is to contemplate some of the spiritual principles you have learned. . . .

Begin by acknowledging the allness of God. . . . God is infinite and fills all space. Realize that the Life that is God is individually expressing Itself as your life. Then rest with that truth and see if you can achieve an absolute conviction of these facts. Let the Presence of God that resides in the midst of you reveal Itself. . . ."

With those words, Mr. Hunt stopped speaking, and we all sat quietly in the warm spring sunlight. After just a few short moments, I felt a gentle sense of peace welling up inside of me, and I was overcome by an absolute awareness of the Divine Presence. It was similar to the sensation I had experienced during the meditation at Shimahn's class in Old Jerusalem. While I was quietly relaxing in this mystical stillness, Pam's voice suddenly broke the silence.

"He's gone!" she shouted. "What happened to him?"

Kathy and I opened our eyes simultaneously after my cousin's outcry. Pam was correct. The three of us were sitting alone on the grass. Mr. Hunt was nowhere in sight!

Chapter Five

For a brief interval after that episode in the park, the two girls and I sat quietly on the grass, hardly saying a word. Each of us had our own personal questions about Mr. Hunt and about the spiritual teaching that he had just shared with us. But, in addition, we each were experiencing a degree of that "peace. . .which passes all understanding"—a tranquil serenity that seems to be achieved only when you are in the presence of a master. Surprisingly, while both of the girls exhibited a remarkable sense of agreement with Mr. Hunt's discourse, Kathy appeared to be especially moved by her meditation experience.

After this period of quiet contemplation, the three of us began slowly walking down the pathway that would take us out of the park. As we walked, Kathy asked, "Eric, why did Mr. Hunt seem to know you? And what was that name that you had asked him about at the beginning of our discussion?"

In answering Kathy's questions, I related the complete story of my adventure with Shimahn and Nehemiah in Old Jerusalem. It was a great relief for me to finally be able to share this experience with someone. The two girls listened intently as I described the incident.

At one point, Pam interrupted by saying, "I remember your mother telling my family about how concerned she was when you disappeared in Jerusalem. Have you ever explained all this to your parents?"

"Nope!" I replied.

When I finished my story, Kathy said, "Gosh, Eric, that certainly must have been an exciting experience for you."

"It really was, Kathy. But looking back now, I must admit that it also has been a bit frustrating. When I first heard Shimahn's message, everything seemed so vibrant and alive for me. But then, after they left me alone in Jerusalem, I felt a deep sense of emptiness. In fact, I have never heard another word about Truth until our encounter with Mr. Hunt today."

Exiting from the park at that point, the three of us abruptly ended our discussion of spiritual matters as we were joined unexpectedly by two of the girls' other friends.

That evening, I lay awake in bed for quite awhile, pondering some of the new concepts that Mr. Hunt had presented to us. But, in addition to thinking about these principles, I was puzzled over the sudden appearance—and disappearance—of this obviously spiritually illumined man.

I had always thought of myself as being a fairly normal person with slightly above-average intelligence and the usual amount of human desires, ambitions, and hopes. Yet I was beginning to wonder if there was some hidden meaning behind these unexplained adventures in mysticism. Were my encounters with Shimahn, Nehemiah, and Mr. Hunt merely accidental, or were these events part of some inexplicable divine plan for me? While I was quite receptive to their message of truth, I also was somewhat confused as to how these principles were to affect my ultimate purpose in life.

On the day after the incident with Mr. Hunt in St. Louis, my parents and I returned to our suburban Chicago home, and I resumed my normal, everyday life in "this world." This was followed by a rather uneventful period of more than three years during which I had no further encounters with any strangers of elevated spiritual consciousness. Yet, while I was not being taught through any outside source during this period, there were several instances when I would recall something that previously had been told to me by either Shimahn, Nehemiah, or Mr. Hunt. And even more important, there were a few times when I would be sitting quietly in meditation, and a new idea would flash into my mind, or I would become aware of some mystical principle that, heretofore, was unknown to me.

Apparently, these things were flowing from the spiritual center of my own being. Was it possible that I was being taught from within by my "real Teacher" who Nehemiah once promised would always be with me?

Inevitably, these incidents occurred when I most needed help in getting through some of the more difficult periods of my teen-age years. But on the whole, these experiences were few and far between and did not always make lasting impressions upon me.

During this period of my life, I also developed a closer relationship with my cousin Pamela, even though we very seldom were in each other's physical presence. Ever since that afternoon in the park with Mr. Hunt, Pam seemed to be drawn to the same Truth that had haunted me for so long. While on the surface her initial response didn't seem as intense as my reaction to Shimahn in Old Jerusalem, I felt that the whole episode had been her breakthrough to a higher understanding of the real nature of existence, and this became the basis for a strong spiritual bond that still exists between us. But while Pam had originally acknowledged a more-than-casual acceptance of these principles, her friend Kathy apparently had undergone a true spiritual awakening as a result of Mr. Hunt's presentation. Kathy's receptivity to the message was quite remarkable. And even though my spiritual nature was extremely impressed by her instantaneous reaction to Truth, my human nature was developing those special yearnings that occur in young boys entering puberty, as I was becoming both physically and emotionally attracted to her. However, after that eventful Easter vacation, I would have only limited opportunities to be with her again.

On the July 4th weekend of the following year, my parents and I flew to St. Louis for a three-day holiday. This trip allowed me to spend a good deal of time with Pam and Kathy. In addition to the usual teen-age frivolity, the three of us became involved in several discussions on spiritual principles. Both of the girls had many questions about mysticism, and in spite of my own limited understanding, I did my best to answer them.

During this visit, there also were a few opportunities for me to be alone with Kathy. The emotions that had been aroused in me a year earlier had grown even stronger on this trip. Kathy was beginning to blossom into a very beautiful young woman. While at times I was almost overcome by this first flush of young love, I tried not to let my feelings be too obvious. In retrospect, I like to believe that Kathy shared my sentiments at that time.

On the final day of this trip, it was quite an emotional moment for me when my parents and I had to leave for the airport for our flight home. During the weeks that followed, I thought about Kathy very often, as I fantasized about the possibility of someday sharing my life with her. However, several months later, I learned from Pam that Kathy's father had just been transferred to a new job in Cincinnati, Ohio. Kathy and her family were moving to the Queen City on the Ohio River, and, like any number of the people we meet in today's transcient society, she was being lifted out of our lives—apparently forever.

Chapter Six

During the next period of my life, time passed quickly, it seemed, and soon I was nearing the end of my high school years. As I began to grow intellectually, I occasionally checked out a religious book from the school library. I was developing an interest in learning about various religions and their attendant philosophies. But I must admit that, other than a few metaphysical writings, none of them made a lasting impression on me, nor did they motivate me to accept their doctrines or beliefs.

Then, during the summer after I had graduated from high school, I was involved in one more unexpected spiritual adventure.

The weeks immediately following my graduation provided me with an abundance of free time. During this period, I had many opportunities for contemplation and meditation. I regularly practiced the spiritual principles that I had learned in the past and, as a result of that activity, achieved an inner realization that I was becoming more and more receptive to Truth. I also experienced an overwhelming premonition that I was about to make a major breakthrough in my attainment of spiritual wisdom.

This intuitive feeling came to fruition late in July of that year, as my continuing mystical initiation reached a new dimension. On a hot, muggy Sunday afternoon, my parents and I boarded an airplane at Chicago's O'Hare Field and flew to San Francisco for another of my father's working vacations.

After lunch on our non-stop flight to California, I decided to relax by listening to some music on the headset that had been passed out to us by our stewardess. With the headset in place, I began dialing the various channels. According to the program listing, the first six channels presented several different types of music, ranging from "classical" and "easy-listening" to "rock" and "country/western". Channel 7 was listed as "blank", channel 8 played Broadway showtunes, and channels 9 and 10 had interviews with well-known politicians and other celebrities.

After listening to some music on channel 5 for about ten minutes, I turned the dial to channel 6. Not being interested in that style of music, I continued moving the dial. As I stopped on channel 7, I heard a familiar male voice speaking with a slight British accent.

The voice said: "'Strait is the gate, and narrow is the way, which leadeth unto life, and few there be that find it.' Only those who are prepared for the spiritual life are called upon. But this preparation is an activity that has been taking place over a period of several lifetimes. If you are one of the 'chosen ones,' you will know it, because when you hear or read statements of absolute Truth, you will feel a oneness with this message, and you will realize that these principles belong to you. You will know that this Truth has always existed within your consciousness and that, by meditating and practicing these principles, you will be 'opening out a way to allow the imprisoned splendor to escape.'"

The voice coming through the headset had caught me completely off guard. In fact, I was so shocked to hear those words that I yanked the earphones from my head and nudged my mother with my elbow. She had been sitting quietly with her eyes closed, listening to some semi-classical music. Because she had been quite relaxed, she obviously was startled when I poked her. With a bit of a frown on her face, she quickly removed her headset and asked:

"What's wrong, Eric?"

"Oh, probably nothing, Mom, but . . . umm, what channel are you listening to?"

Looking at me even more inquisitively, she responded, "Channel 4. . . . Why do you ask?"

"Oh, no reason in particular . . . ah . . . if you don't mind, would you turn to channel 7 and tell me what you hear?"

Placing her earphones back on her head, she dialed number 7 and, after a few seconds, replied, "There's nothing there, Eric, just a little static. In fact, I believe the program lists channel 7 as 'blank'. Is anything wrong?"

"No, Mom! I thought I heard something strange, but I guess I must have had the dial set in the wrong place. . . . I'm sorry!"

Mother gave me one more quick, puzzled glance and then reset her earphones and closed her eyes. Despite the fact that she may not have heard anything on her headset, I was certain that I had just received a spiritual message on mine. I wondered if anyone else in the airplane had had a similar experience. I looked around the cabin at the other passengers seated near me. Several of them were engrossed in rapid conversation; others had their headsets on and were listening to the programmed music; a few had fallen asleep. Everything seemed quite normal in the airplane, so I decided to try to ascertain if I really had heard that voice. Since my dial was still set at channel 7, before putting my headset back in place, I listened through just one earphone which I held a slight distance from my ear. All I heard was a soft static hiss. Somewhat relieved, I put the headset back on and reclined in my seat.

Almost immediately, I heard the same voice say: "Strait is the gate, and narrow is the way, which leadeth unto life," etc. The message that I had received earlier was repeated in its entirety, as if the words had been pre-recorded specifically for me.

Once again, I glanced at my mother, who still was looking very relaxed with her eyes closed. I then gently reached over to the control for her musical program and turned the dial to channel 7. Startled by my unexpected action, she immediately lunged forward in her seat. Then, looking at me angrily, she shouted: "Eric! What's the matter with you?"

"I'm sorry, Mom! I must have turned your dial by mistake."

Giving me one of those disgusted parental looks, she was about to sit back again when I asked, "Uh . . . Mom, what did you hear on channel 7?"

Looking even more exasperated, she said, "I heard static! What did you expect me to hear? There's nothing on that channel."

Shaking her head with one final pained expression on her face, she turned her dial back to channel 4 and closed her eyes as she reclined in her seat.

"What is happening here?" I thought. "Am I the only person on this airplane who can hear that message on channel 7? Maybe there is some flaw in the equipment, and my headset is the only one picking up that broadcast."

I then left my seat and walked back to the area near the washrooms at the rear of the cabin. I lingered there for a few minutes, looking out at the panoramic scene of the majestic Rocky mountains of Western Wyoming. Then, as I was returning to my seat, I asked a stewardess if any musical program was available on channel 7. She told me that the channel was blank at this time, but that, hopefully, there soon would be a program developed for it. Since we were fairly near my seat, I asked if she would check channel 7 on my headset.

After listening for a few moments, she removed the headset, and I anxiously asked, "What did you hear?"

"Nothing," she replied. "All I heard was some static. As I told you, there's nothing on that channel."

"Thank you," I said, as she left to answer a call from another passenger.

After a brief hesitation, I decided to place the earphones on my head, once again, to see if I could discover a possible hidden meaning behind this episode. I made myself comfortable by reclining in my seat, and almost instantaneously the spiritual message was repeated in my headset.

This time, my first reaction was an overwhelming sense of familiarity with the sound of the lecturer's voice. While he never identified himself, the smooth vocal resonance, coupled with that unmistakable trace of a British accent, signaled to me that this Teacher-on-tape was indeed Shimahn—or, if it wasn't Shimahn, the sound certainly was a carbon copy of his voice.

Following that moment of recognition, I more willingly resigned myself to listening to the message. The teacher said: "After Jesus' resurrection from his tomb, he was not observed by many people. Only those of elevated spiritual discernment were able to recognize the risen Christ. In the same way, only those who have been spiritually awakened will be able to comprehend this message."

I could readily agree with that concept, but merely comprehending the message was one thing. Evidently, the people on this airplane were not even capable of hearing the broadcast.

The voice continued: "Spiritual discernment—the activity of 'knowing God aright'—is your access to eternal life. But always remember that God cannot be found in externals. Throughout the centuries, people have been searching for God in holy mountains and in temples made with hands. Yet, Christ Jesus taught that 'the kingdom of God is within you.'

"You may read books on spiritual wisdom, and you may sit at the feet of illumined masters, but you never will be taught of God until you experience the Presence of God that exists within your own consciousness. In those mystical moments of God-realization, you will find the key that unlocks the door to your oneness with Divine Consciousness. This recognition of your unity with the Source of all life will then begin to unfold as the fruitage of your everyday experience, and no longer will you be functioning as the 'natural man.' You will have discovered your real Christ-identity as the spiritual Son of God. Then, like other illumined beings of the past, you, too, will be regarded by mankind as one of those special anointed ones who lives his life as the 'light of the world.'

"In the ancient mystical Gospel we read: 'You have the capacity to rise above all the limitations of this world. Accept your God-given dominion over all things. This is your divine birthright as the image and likeness of Infinite Spirit. Thou art the Christ, the Son of the living God.'

"Accept this divine birthright! Acknowledge your Christhood, and your life will be lived in a new, higher dimension of consciousness."

The teacher paused for just a moment, and then he said: "The next several days will be a very exciting period for you. You are about to embark on a unique spiritual journey. A great mystical discovery awaits you in the 'City by the Bay.'

"Jesus promised to make his followers 'fishers of men.' When you first enter the realm of the fishermen, you will assume that you have come to the end of your search for absolute Truth. But, soon, you will discover that your new-found treasure is really just 'the beginning'."

I had no idea what that was supposed to mean and, before I could analyze those last statements, the speaker concluded his discourse:

"Now turn within yourself in silent contemplation and ponder these significant truths. Let the indwelling Presence of God reveal Itself. Allow your real Christ-identity to take over your experience and live Its life *in, as, and through* you."

After that injunction the teacher stopped speaking and all I heard in my headset was a soft static hiss. I wanted to follow his directive to meditate, but I was quite puzzled by this entire incident.

Was the voice in fact Shimahn's? Was this recorded message prepared exclusively for me? While much of the teaching was primarily a reiteration of spiritual principles that I had heard in the past, there also was the implication that another mystical adventure awaited me in San Francisco. And what did the teacher mean when he spoke about the "realm of the fishermen?"

After dwelling on these questions for awhile, I decided to meditate on the truth I had just heard. I removed the headset, closed my eyes and directed my attention to the inner sanctuary of my being, as I tried to become aware of the Presence of God within me. Very quickly, I achieved a deep sense of harmonious quietude and was able to rest in that meditative state until the silence was broken by the captain's voice announcing that he was making preparations for our landing at San Francisco's International Airport.

Chapter Seven

After claiming our baggage at the airport, my parents and I hired a taxi which took us to the legendary Palace Hotel on Market Street in downtown San Francisco. After checking into the Palace, we ate a sumptuous dinner in the hotel's renowned Garden Court restaurant and then spent the balance of the evening relaxing in our suite. During the next two days, we toured many of the city's famous landmarks. Among these were Telegraph Hill and the Coit Tower, Union Square, Chinatown, the Palace of Fine Arts and, finally, the Golden Gate Bridge and its environs.

On the fourth day of our trip, my father had to attend several business meetings at one of the large downtown hotels, so my mother and I decided to take a cable-car ride to Fisherman's Wharf.

After spending about an hour together in the wharf area, it became evident that Mother and I did not share the same interests in shopping and sight-seeing. She was hoping to find some special bargains in clothing for herself, and she also wanted to purchase some unique household items and other trinkets that she could take home as souvenirs for several of her friends.

I was more interested in seeing the various artists at work and in searching through the back streets and out-of-the-way shops for any hidden treasures that I might discover. So Mother and I agreed to split up and go our separate ways, with the understanding that we would meet again at three p.m. near the point where we could reboard our cable car.

After browsing for awhile in several different arts and crafts shops, I gradually drifted down to the waterfront area where many of the fishing boats were docked. Near the end of one of the piers, I paused briefly and allowed my attention to be drawn to a rather small wooden boat that was quite disordered and obviously in need of extensive repairs and maintenance.

Inside the boat, a weather-beaten old man was huddled in a corner, working on some of his fishing lines and other equipment. He had a corncob pipe in his mouth and several days' growth of gray stubble on his face.

After I had been standing there watching him for a few moments, he glanced up at me and squinted as he pushed his spectacles up onto his forehead, trying to scrutinize me better. I couldn't help but laugh out loud at the sight of this strange little man. He looked exactly as you would expect Popeye the Sailor Man to look at age seventy-five.

This crusty old fisherman then removed the pipe from his mouth and his face broke into a wide grin, which made him look even more ridiculous. He had only four or five teeth, all spaced at strategic intervals across the front of his mouth.

"Can I help you, young feller?" he asked.

"No! I'm just browsing around the area," I replied.

"You're not the young man from Jerusalem, are you?"

"No, I'm from Chicago."

After answering so nonchalantly, I suddenly became rather perplexed. But also, I was overcome by a mysterious sense of intrigue, as I gave his question a second thought. "Was I the young man from Jerusalem?" I wondered if I had given him the proper answer.

"Why do you ask about someone from Jerusalem?" I inquired.

Pointing a finger to the wharf area on my left, he answered, "Because they told me that if a young feller from Jerusalem came by, I should send him down to the little shop at the end of that alley along the waterfront."

Recalling the final words that I had heard on my headset in the airplane, I wondered if this "old man of the sea" was to play a part in my promised spiritual adventure in the "City by the Bay."

After that bit of hesitation, I continued our conversation: "Uh, excuse me sir, but do you know Shimahn?"

"What's a Shimahn?" he asked, as he pulled his glasses down from his forehead and resumed working on his fishing equipment.

Becoming even more intrigued by this situation, I then questioned, "Who did you say told you to watch for a young man from Jerusalem?"

"I didn't say! But since you ask . . . a couple of Arab fellers came by yesterday and gave me twenty dollars. They said I should send some young man from Jerusalem down to that shop in the corner of the alley."

"What kind of shop is it?"

"Beats me," he said. "I didn't even know there was a shop down there."

I then asked, "How long have you been fishing in this area?"

"'Bout fifty-seven years," he replied.

"Thank you," I said, as I turned away from him and began walking along the dock toward the alley.

As I approached the entrance to the alley, I heard the old fisherman shout at me: "Hey. . . ! Are you him?"

I spun around and faced him, as he said, "You know... are you the young feller from Jerusalem?"

I really didn't know the answer to that question, so I just shrugged my shoulders as I turned away from him and continued walking into the alley.

The alley was quite narrow—about ten feet across—and the footpath consisted of a few bricks and large stones mixed in with some gravel. Most of the buildings on either side of the walkway were vacant and in a state of total disrepair. If these buildings had been located in Chicago, the city zoning department, no doubt, would have condemned them and, probably, would have had them razed within a few weeks.

As I moved along, I heard no sounds and soon realized that the area was quite deserted. After walking the equivalent of about two city blocks, I approached the end of the alley. A short distance from the end, set back about twelve feet on the left side of the walkway, was an ornately carved door offering entrance to a quaint little shop whose facade was decorated in a unique nautical theme. The shop was not visible until you reached a point almost directly in front of the door, and there were no conspicuous signs, directories, or other advertisements in the area to announce the shop's existence.

However, as I approached the building, I noticed a small hand-carved wooden plaque just above the door. On it were the words:

"Fishermen's Realm," I thought. "Why does that sound familiar. . . ? Of course . . . the voice on the airplane had said: 'When you enter the realm of the fishermen . . .' and then he continued with something about my not being at the end of my search but at the beginning."

My heart began to pound in my chest as I reached for the doorknob. What spiritual adventure awaited me inside? Was I to meet another enlightened teacher of mysticism?

Just before opening the door, my mind quickly conjured up visions of what might be on the other side. I visualized a dark, intimate little shop with a few strange-looking people sitting in meditation and possibly a few Arabs lurking in dark corners. Maybe there would even be a Hindu snake charmer plying his trade. I also assumed that the entire room would be filled with smoke and would be imbued with the aroma of burning incense.

Instead, as I opened the door, I was stunned by the obvious normalcy of what I saw. Here was a brightly lit showroom that was much larger than it appeared from outside and was manned by several collegiate-looking sales clerks. All the walls were filled with books, and the tables and showcases throughout the center of the room were covered with very commonplace, nautical-oriented gifts and souvenirs.

Even more surprising was the clientele. There were more than thirty customers walking up and down the aisles.

"Where did all these people come from?" I wondered. "How did they all find this place?" There was no one in the alley when I came in. And I was quite astonished—but at the same time a little disappointed—by the fact that all the customers looked like typical tourists.

Even though the atmosphere of the shop wasn't exactly what I had expected, I nonetheless began wandering up and down the aisles, browsing through the souvenirs and other collectibles. I kept looking over my shoulder in anticipation, waiting for some mysterious stranger to approach me. One elderly woman mistook me for a sales clerk and began asking questions about an old compass that was on display. I excused myself by explaining that I, too, was a customer.

After about twenty minutes of no activity and no surprises, I began to feel a bit let down. Everything in the store seemed too normal. Apparently, it was just another day of business as usual.

I then began looking through the massive display of reading material. Virtually every shelf in the store was jammed full of books, and in some cases there were volumes lying horizontally on top of those that were standing upright.

Following my usual routine in book stores, I quickly drifted into the area specializing in religious and philosophical writings. As I was browsing through that section, my eyes were attracted to one specific shelf near the middle of the department. While all the other bookcases in the store were completely full, this particular shelf was totally empty, except for a single black leather book standing alone at the center of the shelf.

Standing there like a soldier at attention, the little black book literally screamed for my recognition. I stepped closer to the case and removed the book as I glanced at the title. My heart almost leaped into my throat as I saw the words: "THE GOSPEL According to 'I AM'".

"My God!" I thought. "Can this be Shimahn's little book?"

I quickly opened it to the Table of Contents. The book was divided into various subjects. There were titles such as: "CREATION (Spiritual Unfoldment)" — "IDENTITY (The Son of God & The Son of Man)" — "REALITY AND ILLUSION (My Kingdom and This World)" — "GOOD AND EVIL (The Pairs of Opposites)" — "PRAYER (Meditation and Communion)" — "SPIRITUAL HEALING", etc.

I then skimmed through some of the subjects in that section of the book. I discovered that each heading was followed by a compilation of relevant Scriptural passages. These quotations were summarized in a mystical interpretation by the author or authors of this book.

Thrilled by what, to me, was a monumental discovery, I carried the book to the checkout counter at the front of the store. Before ringing up the sale, the checkout clerk copied a number off the book's price tag and began looking through a large index file. After several minutes of combing the file, the clerk turned toward me with a puzzled frown on his face.

"Is anything wrong?" I asked.

"Probably not," he said. "It's just that each time we sell a book, we must subtract that sale from the particular book's inventory card. By doing that, we are able to keep a record of how quickly certain items are selling, and we also know when to reorder the publication. . . . My problem here is that I can't find an inventory card for the book you wish to purchase. In fact, I don't recall ever seeing this book before."

"Well, I'm sure the card will turn up. Your price tag indicates a cost of eight dollars and ninety-five cents. Here is a ten-dollar bill."

"I'm sorry sir, but I'll have to call my manager."

The clerk summoned his superior via an intercom system connected to his telephone. In less than a minute, the manager joined us at the counter. Fortunately, there were no other customers in the checkout line at that time.

After the clerk explained his problem, the manager said, "I don't understand. . . ! Every book in this store has an inventory card. Otherwise it can't be placed on our display shelves."

The manager then looked through the index but he, too, could not find an inventory card. He then asked the clerk to check the title page of the book to see who was listed there as publisher.

"There is no publisher listed," replied the clerk.

"Well, under whose name is the copyright notice?"

"I'm sorry, Ken, but there is no copyright notice."

"That's impossible. . . ! No book could be published without a copyright notice!"

I then interrupted their conversation. "Gentlemen, it's entirely possible that the title page and copyright notice have merely been torn out of the book, and I'm sure you'll eventually find the missing inventory card. . . . Now this is your company's price tag, is it not?"

"Yes!" they replied in unison.

"All right, then . . . here is my money! Now please give me my change along with a cash register receipt, and I'll be on my way."

The two men looked at each other curiously as the manager shrugged his shoulders and told the clerk to ring up the sale. As I was walking toward the exit, I heard one of them comment about probably having trouble reordering the book.

Needless to say, now that I finally had found Shimahn's little book, I was quite anxious to get back to the hotel so I could start digging in to my newfound treasure. In all the years since my introduction to mysticism back in Old Jerusalem, I had received all my instruction via the spoken word. Now, for the first time, I would be able to read and study about Truth. I had acquired a virtual textbook of spiritual principles.

As I left the shop and stepped back out into the alley, I once again was overcome by the almost eerie silence. Unlike the noisy hustle and bustle of the showroom, the alley was just as deserted as it had been when I had passed through it earlier. No one was coming or going.

Exiting from the alley, I walked back down to the end of the pier so I could say goodbye to the old fisherman. Arriving at the place where his boat had been anchored, I was quite surprised to discover that neither he nor his vessel were there. It was too late in the day for him to have gone fishing and, considering the ramshackle condition of his boat, it didn't appear that he could travel very far without sinking.

While I was standing there, another larger craft pulled up to the pier and docked itself in the stall next to the spot where the old fisherman had been parked. As the four-man crew disembarked from their boat, I approached the rugged-looking sailor who seemed to be in charge.

"Good afternoon, sir," I greeted him. "I'm looking for the old fisherman who docks his boat next to yours."

"I'm sorry, kiddo, but nobody docks a boat there. That spot's been vacant for more than two years now."

"But he was parked there a little while ago. In fact, he sent me down to the shop at the end of that alley along the waterfront."

"What shop at the enda the alley?" he asked, with a puzzled frown on his face. He then turned to his crewmembers and shouted, "Hey, mates. . . ! Have any of you sea dogs ever seen a boat docked next to us here?"

They all laughed and shook their heads, as they mumbled some negative responses under their breath.

The crew chief then asked, "Do anya you old salts know anything about a shop down at the enda that alley?"

Again they all made noises and gestures in the negative.

Looking back at me, the head fisherman condescendingly said, "Sorry, kid! Are you sure yer in the right city? If you been seein' sailors and boats and shops that ain't there, you musta been out in the sun too long."

His three crewmembers immediately joined him in raucous laughter as I subconsciously squeezed my new book just to be certain it was still there. . . . It was! But by that time, I was beginning to wonder if that nautical bookstore really did exist. I considered going back through the alley just to check but, glancing down at my wrist watch, I suddenly realized that it was five minutes to three. I'd have to hurry if I didn't want to leave my mother waiting at the cable-car stop. Fortunately, she, too, had become quite engrossed in her shopping spree, and even though I was a few minutes late, we arrived simultaneously at our agreed-upon meeting place.

"Hi, Mom!" I greeted her.

"Oh, Hello, Eric! Did you have a nice time?"

"Not too bad, Mom."

She then said, "I hope your afternoon was as exciting as mine. I discovered some of the most unusual shops. Were you able to find any rare treasures? Did you buy anything?"

"Oh, I saw quite a few interesting souvenirs and artifacts, but all I bought was a book."

"A book. . . ? Oh, Eric, what a waste of time. You can buy books every day of the week in Chicago. When you're in a cosmopolitan city like San Francisco, you should do something unique and exotic."

We boarded our cable car as she continued to lecture me: "We come to a place as stimulating as Fisherman's Wharf in San Francisco, and instead of delving into the colorful atmosphere of the area, you spend your time in a typical bookstore."

I just nodded my head in resignation as our cable car began climbing the steep hill south of the wharf area. I was able to get Mother's mind off this subject as I pointed to the magnificent view of the waterfront, with the infamous Alcatraz prison complex sitting so isolated in the middle of the bay.

After returning to our suite at the Palace Hotel, I quietly retired to my room and began reading "THE GOSPEL". Never before had I seen Scriptural truths explained so logically. Grouped under specific topical headings, the Bible verses just seemed to flow from one to another. It was as though the author of this book had been able to uncover the profound spiritual secrets of the ages—secrets that always had been ubiquitously present in the Bible—and, then, by presenting a mystical interpretation of the Biblical passages, had made it possible for anyone to understand the esoteric meaning of the Scriptures.

I continued reading. As my eyes skimmed the pages and my mind absorbed the words, an extraordinary feeling came over me. After scanning no more than fifteen or sixteen pages, I felt a great desire to pause and meditate.

While doing this, it occurred to me that I was in complete agreement with every word that I had read. But more than just agreeing with the ideas being imparted there, I realized that I already knew all those words! I was innately aware of the principles being presented.

What a unique experience to feel that oneness with the written word and with the consciousness that brought it forth!

As I continued studying "THE GOSPEL According to 'I AM'", it became apparent that the mystical Truth in this little book was not being given to me from outside my own being, but what I was seeing in print was actually my own consciousness expressed as form. This was not something that I had just acquired. Rather, it was the "Word of God" that had been revealing Itself within me through the years since my spiritual awakening. I realized that what I was seeing on the printed page was nothing else but my own consciousness expressing itself in an outward form that I could perceive and understand.

Chapter Eight

Later that same evening, I continued perusing "THE GOSPEL According to 'I AM'". I soon discovered that, while the book places a great emphasis on the infinitude of God, there also is a good deal of copy devoted to what the author calls "the nature of error."

When Gautama the Buddha was searching to find reasons for sickness, old age and death, he came to the realization that all these negative aspects of life are "maya" or "illusion". While that philosophy was set forth more than twenty-five-hundred years ago, it truly has not become a part of the consciousness of mankind. As a consequence, we continue to live under the influence of many physical and mental laws. Apparently, sickness, old age and death still are destined to play their roles in our human experience.

However, resurrecting and reviving this ancient tenet, "THE GOSPEL" teaches that these so-called laws of matter appear to have power over us *only when we accept the illusion* of a three-dimensional, materialistic sense of existence. By virtue of our having been born into this conceptual world, we have allowed ourselves to be dominated by an impersonal, universal belief in two powers. But we have the capacity to rise above this illusory sense into a fourth-dimensional, spiritual state of consciousness. Functioning at that higher level of awareness, we can demonstrate that physical laws have no power in our experience. As we acknowledge and accept our oneness with the Source of all Life, we bring ourselves into conformity with God's laws. In those moments of mystical union, we set aside the counterfeit laws of "this world."

The result of this activity of consciousness is the revelation of our true identity as the perfect and complete manifestation of God's Own Being. Outwardly, this then may appear as what mankind refers to as healing. It may unfold as the dissolution of a disease, the overcoming of a financial lack, or the correction of a problem in human relationships. But, whatever the outer form may be, it is the inner mystical realization that brings about the harmonious circumstances or conditions.

This concept of spiritual healing was a rather startling new idea for me. At first I thought it quite incredible that physical diseases and other human problems could be dissolved through mental or spiritual treatment. I didn't recall that Shimahn had ever mentioned the subject of healing in his classwork.

"And yet," I thought, "wouldn't spiritual healing be a natural derivative of a philosophy that reveals the infinite allness of God and the illusory nature, or nothingness, of things pertaining to this physical realm of cause and effect?"

The spiritual ministries of both Gautama the Buddha and Christ Jesus received much of their impetus from the healing works performed by these two highly illumined men. The Bible narratives, which describe some of the cures brought about through the Christ-consciousness of Jesus, illustrate how the people of his time reacted to these events. Most of those who witnessed Jesus' ministry thought of him as being either a magician or a person who had been divinely vested with some miraculous curative powers. But notwithstanding the various opinions of the general populace, it was the spiritual healing work of the Master that gave living proof to his message and, thereby, attracted many of his followers.

Jesus realized that he did not possess some unique, super-human power that made it possible for him to perform miracles. This was not a special dispensation in which the laws of nature were set aside for one brief moment in the long and continuing history of mankind.

Any healings brought about through the enlightened consciousness of Jesus were not miracles. These events did not negate any real laws but were performed in perfect consonance with the laws of God. The only things that were nullified were the false beliefs of this physical sense of existence. That is why the Master told us: "He that believeth on me, the works that I do shall he do also; and greater works than these shall he do."

Jesus knew that, in his healing work, he was applying specific principles—principles which made it possible for him to see through the illusion of physical-sense testimony. Accordingly, he further realized that any of his followers who understood these same principles could also rise to that level of awareness in which they, too, could perceive ultimate reality. Then, through this activity of awakened consciousness, they would be able to emulate the Master's works: "the works that I do shall he do also."

But while it is possible for anyone to achieve "that mind which was also in Christ Jesus," we soon discover that the process of developing a healing consciousness can be the work of several lifetimes.

When I first read through the chapter on spiritual healing in "THE GOSPEL According to 'I AM'", I very quickly saw the logic in the principles that were presented there. I had undergone an almost instantaneous intellectual acceptance of the Letter of Truth. But as Nehemiah had told me during our final discussion in Old Jerusalem, our real goal should be to attain a conscious awareness of the Spirit of Truth; and this, in turn, will function as the Presence and Power that maintains, sustains and enriches our life.

Needless to say, my discovery and acquisition of Shimahn's little book was the high point of my trip to San Francisco. On the days after the episode on Fisherman's Wharf, my parents and I crossed the Golden Gate Bridge to visit the quaint community of Sausalito, and then we toured the famous Muir Woods National Monument. Because of my preoccupation with my new book of spiritual wisdom, however, even the majesty of the magnificent redwoods made little impact upon me.

This memorable vacation in the "City by the Bay" was concluded on the following Sunday morning. Our return flight to Chicago departed as scheduled and was quite uneventful. Incidentally, as soon as our flight was airborne, I plugged in my headset and turned the dial to Channel 7. Though the program directory still listed the channel as blank, my headset was filled with the sound of religious and gospel music. I asked a stewardess about this, and she told me that a new gospel music tape had been added but the printed program had not yet been updated to indicate the change. Apparently, no further mystical adventures were in store for me at that time.

The period immediately following our return from San Francisco was quite restful, and I was able to spend a good deal of time studying my new "GOSPEL". I was fortunate to have had that opportunity to work with the spiritual principles, because the following September I enrolled as a full-time student at Purdue University in West Lafayette, Indiana, and soon was completely engrossed in campus life and my academic studies.

That first year of college was an exciting experience for me as I gained a new sense of independence. This was the first time that I had been away from my parents for a prolonged period. Also, I made a number of new friends and, as the year progressed, became very involved in school activities.

Inevitably, each person who has discovered Truth and, therefore, has embarked upon his personal spiritual journey, will be tempted by many distractions of "this world." Quite often we become thoroughly absorbed in these distractions and allow ourselves to be sidetracked from making progress on the "path".

During my first year at the university, I was no exception to this rule. Campus life provided me with many new challenges. And as I struggled to survive both academically and socially, my attention was constantly being directed away from the mystical principles that I had learned. In fact, though I had brought my copy of "THE GOSPEL According to 'I AM'" to my new living quarters at the university, I spent very little time reading the book.

In relation to my school activities and responsibilities, the spiritual life, at times, seemed to be little more than an interesting diversion. Apparently there are very few of us who, in our early stages of spiritual development, will diligently practice the principles, especially if our life is going along smoothly. In many cases it takes a serious problem or other traumatic experience to "drive" us into the spirit.

I had one of those learning experiences late in the following school year. I was alone in my dormitory one afternoon when I received an alarming telephone call from my mother.

Her voice was shaking as she said: "Eric, please catch the next bus home! Your dad just had a severe heart attack!"

"Oh, Mom! How is he? Will he be all right?"

"The doctors say it's very 'touch and go' right now. He's in intensive care. Please come home as soon as you can!" And before I could say another word, there was an abrupt silence and then an ominous, prolonged dial tone.

Though my heart was pounding intensely as I hurriedly packed some essentials into a small travel bag, I felt a sudden impulse to also take along my copy of "THE GOSPEL". I placed the book in the pocket of my sport coat, to keep it readily accessible, and rushed off to the Greyhound bus terminal.

The bus ride to Chicago was very difficult for me. A lifetime of experiences flashed through my mind and, in addition, all the usual questions: "Why my father? He is a good man. He's always been in good health. . . . Should I try to meditate? Can I reach the silence and feel some peace? Why haven't I worked more with the spiritual principles?" At a time like that I felt so inadequate.

Arriving in Chicago, I took a taxi from the bus depot directly to the hospital. As I entered the intensive care unit, my mother saw me through her tears and came down the hall to meet me in an emotional scene. She then took my hand and escorted me to the bed where my father was lying under an oxygen tent. His eyes were closed and his skin was colorless. It was the most shocking experience of my young life . . . I felt so helpless.

After several hours of silent vigil at my father's bedside, I excused myself and went downstairs to the hospital lobby. Just off the main reception area was a small non-denominational chapel. I entered the dimly-lit room and, seeing that no one else was there, just sat quietly for awhile with my eyes closed. I tried to recall some of the statements of truth that I had learned in the past. Though I wanted to help my father, I realized that I couldn't be of help to anyone unless I could get some peace within myself.

After sitting in silent contemplation for a few minutes, I opened my little book to the chapter on "Spiritual Healing". In that chapter, I saw the words: "Healing is revealing! Allow the spiritual Son of God—the Christ which you really are—to reveal Itself at the center of your being. That revelation of true identity, then, will function as the restoration of harmony to any discordant appearances that have been presented to you. Always remember that you have no power to heal anything! But when you touch the Christ within you, It can operate through you and will go before you to 'make the crooked places straight'."

I sat there for more than an hour, alternately reading several paragraphs in "THE GOSPEL" and then quietly contemplating the truth that I had read. At one point in my meditations, I realized that my father did not live because of the functions of his physical body. I saw that the issues of his life were not dependent upon that body, but that he, as the individualized expression of God's Being, really had a spiritual nature. His true identity—his very life itself—was the Divine Consciousness appearing in an individual form; and that identity could never die.

After realizing those truths, my mind became quiet as I "rested in the Word." I have no idea how long I lingered in that silence, but at one point I was startled somewhat as I heard the words within me: "'Call no man your father upon the earth: for One is your Father, which is in heaven.' Therefore your Father's Life is immortal and eternal . . . *I* am that Life . . . *I* am the Life of all being."

After hearing those words, I gradually was overcome by an indescribable sense of peace and harmony. I felt as though my entire being was now at one with all life and that I was immersed in an all-encompassing sea of universal Divine Love.

Shortly thereafter, I found my mind drifting back to the events of "this world." But while I had allowed myself to once again be *in* the world, I also realized that, as a result of my deep meditation, I would not have to be *of* the world.

Rising from the pew, I walked to the elevator which would take me back to the intensive care ward. Strangely, I no longer felt the deep concern for my father's well-being.

As I approached the area near his bed, my mother came up to me and clutched my hand, but this time she was smiling through her tears.

"Eric, where were you? He's going to be all right! The doctors told me that your dad has passed the crisis. He's sitting up in his bed and wants to see you."

Chapter Nine

My father's recovery from his heart attack was quite remarkable. In fact, one of his doctors used the term "miraculous" in describing his rapid return to normalcy. While the initial prognosis indicated that there would be severe muscle and tissue damage, later tests showed that this did not materialize. Within a few weeks, my father was given a clean bill of health and was allowed to return to his work.

Was I an instrument for his healing? An impartial observer might claim that my father's rapid recovery was merely a coincidence, or was a result of his previous good physical condition. That may be true! However, since that time, I have witnessed many events which would testify to the healing power of a spiritually enlightened consciousness—a mind imbued with Truth. But even more important, as a direct result of the experience with my father, I was motivated to spend more time "Practicing the Presence of God" and working to gain a higher level of spiritual awareness. As I did this, I found that my scholastic work began to improve, and other activities in my outer life became more harmonious.

By my third year at the university, I had become quite acclimated to the college lifestyle. I was able to keep my grades at a respectable level and, at the same time, maintain a fairly active social life. During the previous two-and-one-half years, I had dated four different girls for varying lengths of time. Yet, even though I was always quite selective before even dating a girl, none of those relationships ever reached a point that could have been classified as serious.

Then one afternoon in the spring of that year, I was leaving the Student Union Building when I paused before the bulletin board in the lobby. On the board were many announcements of upcoming campus events. Slightly hidden by the other papers was a powder-blue copy of a handwritten flyer which read:

ANNOUNCING

A Tape Recorded Lecture On

PRINCIPLES OF
PRIMITIVE
CHRISTIAN
MYSTICISM

Learn the
Spiritual Secrets of the Ages...

Tuesday, April 9th
at 7:30 p.m.
at
Elizabeth Fowler Hall

"'Primitive Christian Mysticism'? What's that supposed to mean?" I wondered. Since this was Friday, April 5th, the lecture was to be held in just four days. For some unexplained reason, the speaker's name did not appear on the announcement, and there was no indication as to which campus organization was sponsoring the event. Nonetheless, my curiosity had been aroused, and I certainly would make every effort to attend the meeting.

Even if the speaker presented a different approach to mysticism from that to which I was accustomed, this would be a good opportunity for me to meet other students on the "path". Obviously, on a campus as large as Purdue University's, there must be hundreds of students who would have an interest in learning about Truth.

On the following Tuesday evening, I made a point of arriving early at the lecture hall. I wanted to be assured of a good seat. As I approached the entrance, I saw an extremely attractive young woman standing in the doorway, waiting to greet the visitors. She had strikingly beautiful blond hair that was cut to a length slightly below her shoulders and, even from a distance, she radiated a healthy wholesome vitality. This girl could easily have been one of those models who appear in televised soap and shampoo commercials, or in any other advertisement in which the producer tries to convey an image of freshness and beauty.

As I came near, she smiled enthusiastically and handed me what appeared to be a powder-blue program.

"Hi! Welcome to our lecture," she greeted me.

"Thank you," I replied, as I accepted the piece of paper which turned out to be the same as the announcement that had been posted on the bulletin board in the Student Union.

We both paused momentarily as we gazed at each other for a brief interval. Her eyes were a deep brown color, a rather unique characteristic for a girl with such fair skin and warm-toned, natural blond hair. As we stared at each other for that fleeting moment, I felt a strong sense of familiarity toward her.

Though I had been dating girls for several years, I still was a bit shy in the presence of the opposite sex—especially at a first encounter. And this young lady wasn't making it easy for me. She never dropped her gaze. She was able to look me straight in the eyes until my cheeks became flushed.

I bashfully looked away from her as I softly mumbled "Thank you" again. Entering the meeting room, I discovered that I was the first person to have arrived for the lecture.

Elizabeth Fowler Hall was one of the most popular meeting rooms on the campus. With theater-style seating, the hall had a capacity of about one-hundred-seventy-five people. At the front of the room was a rather primitive reel-to-reel tape recorder standing upright on a small table. I wondered if that machine was indicative of the so-called "Primitive Christian Mysticism" that I soon would be learning about.

I took a seat in the first row and tried to look relaxed. Why did this girl seem so familiar? I glanced toward the doorway and saw that she was looking over her shoulder, staring at me. This time she smiled meekly and quickly turned away when I looked at her.

After awhile, I checked the time on my wrist watch. It was seven-twenty-five. Fifteen minutes had passed and no one else had entered the room. During that period, I had been trying to look preoccupied and aloof, but with nothing else to keep me busy, I read through the lecture announcement approximately seventeen times.

Five minutes later, the girl in the doorway came into the room and turned on the tape recorder. Apparently this relic of a machine needed to warm up before it could be played.

Standing in front of the table, the attractive young lady turned toward me and began to announce the program. She appeared amazingly cool and unruffled by the fact that I was the only person in attendance. Acting as if she were addressing a large audience, she said:

"Good evening! And welcome to our lecture on Primitive Christian Mysticism. We're certain you'll find this to be an interesting presentation."

She then pushed the "forward" button on the recorder and smiled at me as she seated herself in the third chair to my left. Evidently the tape had an extremely long leader, because a loud hissing sound was coming from the machine. For a moment, I thought the old tape recorder might explode.

I fought to control myself from laughing out loud. But, also, I was beginning to feel a bit sorry for this beautiful girl who seemed so sincere about this presentation. She certainly had gone through a good deal of work in making the preparations. Yet, if I hadn't come, she would have received no response to her announcement. I wondered where the other members of her organization were.

I glanced at her, sitting there three seats away from me. She was looking straight ahead, patiently waiting for the lecture to begin. Then I heard that familiar voice say the words:

"'Strait is the gate, and narrow is the way, which leadeth unto life, and few there be that find it.' Only those who are prepared for the spiritual life are called upon. But this preparation is an activity that has been taking place over a period of several lifetimes. If you are one of the 'chosen ones', you will know it, because when you hear or read statements of absolute Truth, you will feel a oneness with this message, and you will realize that these principles belong to you," etc.

I couldn't believe my ears! This was the same speech that I had heard on the airplane during my trip to San Francisco. Where in the world did she get this tape?

I listened to the message for another five minutes until I could no longer control myself. Churning inside, I abruptly rose from my seat, walked up to the table and turned off the recorder. Somewhat startled by my unexpected action, the young lady looked at me inquiringly as I said:

"I'm sorry, but I had to interrupt this. . . . Where did you get this tape?"

"Why do you ask?"

"Because I've heard it before. Please . . . this is important to me. Where did you get it?"

"I received it in the mail."

"Okay, I understand that. But who produced it? Who did you order it from?"

"I didn't order it. It just came to me in the mail."

"What do you mean, 'it just came to you?'" I shouted. "Are you telling me that you merely were sitting there in your living room one day, and the mailman came by and just dropped off this tape for you?"

"Yes!"

"Come on! You certainly don't expect me to believe that, do you?"

"it doesn't matter if you believe it or not. It just happens to be the truth!"

This conversation was getting me more confused by the minute. I then asked: "Where did the tape come from? Did you notice the return address?"

"There was no return address. It came in a plain brown wrapper."

"Well, do you know the name of the lecturer?"

"No!" she answered.

"Don't you even care who he is?"

"Of course I care!" she replied. "But I have not been able to learn his name. Now if you don't mind, I'd like to hear the rest of this lecture. Please turn the recorder back on!"

I hesitated for a moment and then said, "Surely, you must have heard this lecture before."

"Yes, several times!"

"Well that's good, because I've heard it too! So why don't we just forget the tape and go someplace where we can talk for awhile?"

She stood up and rather indignantly said: "Listen here! This is a scheduled campus activity. We're supposed to be listening to a taped lecture on Principles of Primitive Christian Mysticism, and I would like to finish the tape!"

"But we've both heard it before!"

She then said: "You must be a new student of mysticism! Because if you had any background, you'd realize that we don't go to a lecture just to hear the words! The words may be interesting, but they only constitute the 'Letter of Truth.' The important point of these meetings is that we achieve an awareness of the 'Spirit of Truth.' We came here tonight in order to have a mystical experience— to recognize the Christ of God that dwells deep within our soul. If you don't understand something as basic as that, then you shouldn't have come. Now, will you please turn on the recorder?"

What could I say? She was absolutely correct! But she couldn't have hurt me more if she had slapped me in the face. And how about her mystical vocabulary? The words flowed from her mouth as if Shimahn were speaking through her.

I pushed the "forward" button on the tape recorder and sheepishly walked back to my seat. As I sat down, I noticed that she was watching me. Catching my eye, she smiled and gently nodded her head toward me, as if to send a silent "Thank you."

The teacher continued. But, unlike my experience on the airplane, when the speaker on this tape came to the point where he had previously told me of my upcoming adventure in San Francisco, in this lecture, he merely continued with his mystical message. My earlier conviction that this voice belonged to Shimahn was reinforced by the fact that the last half hour of this discourse was almost identical to Shimahn's classwork in Old Jerusalem.

While I had many questions about the tape that I was hearing, I was even more intrigued by the beautiful young woman seated to my left. I didn't recall ever having seen a girl with as much natural beauty—maybe in the movies, but never in person. And in addition to her good looks, she obviously was a student of spiritual Truth. But she also displayed a strange zealousness about her "Primitive Christian Mysticism." How did she ever come up with that name for the teaching? And had she prepared that night's meeting all by herself, or was she a part of some larger group of students?

I glanced at her several times during the speech. Every now and then it appeared that she had been scrutinizing me until I looked in her direction, at which time she would quickly turn away. Then, after we had been listening to the tape for about forty minutes, she suddenly rose from her seat, walked up to the table, and turned off the recorder. I wondered what to expect next from this "lady of mystery" as she slowly came toward me and sat down in the chair right next to mine.

Looking directly at me with those warm brown eyes, she said, "I think I owe you an apology."

Taken aback by that statement, I replied, "No, it was my fault. I shouldn't have turned off the machine."

"That's not important now. I was wrong to imply that you didn't know anything about mysticism. With your background, I'm sure you're aware of mystical principles that I have never even heard of."

Now what was she talking about? What did she know about my background?

She then said, "When I first saw you approach the doorway tonight, I felt that you looked familiar, even though you were out of place. And now I know why. . . . Your name's Eric, isn't it?"

"Yes," I replied with a curious frown on my face.

When I showed no sign of recognition she said, "Oh, Eric, was I that forgettable? Don't you remember me at all...? I'm Kathy, your cousin Pam's old friend."

"Oh, gosh, Kathy . . . is it really you?" I asked, as I reached for her hand.

Was it possible that this gorgeous young woman was that same sweet girl that I had felt so strongly about when I was fourteen years old?

"I can't believe it, Eric . . . after all these years. . . ."

She leaned over and kissed my cheek.

We just quietly stared at each other for a few moments, and then she said, "Well, what do you think? Do you want to hear the rest of the tape?"

I replied, "Frankly, if you don't mind, I'd rather not. *You* have been enough of a mystical experience for one evening. I'm afraid I wouldn't be a very good listener at this point."

Smiling at me, Kathy took her hand from mine and walked up to the table, where she began rewinding the tape. I couldn't take my eyes off of her. All those emotions that I had felt for her seven years ago were instantaneously brought back to life in me. I wanted to reach out and hold her in my arms, so that she wouldn't be able to disappear from me again. And there were so many questions that I wanted to ask her. We definitely had much to talk about.

Kathy locked the old tape recorder in a cabinet at the front of the lecture hall. As the two of us walked out of the room, I asked, "Was this meeting tonight exclusively your idea, or are you part of a larger group?"

"Nobody else was involved," she said. "It was completely my own show."

"I'm sorry that you didn't get a better response."

"It was the best response I have ever had. The last three times nobody showed up, so I just sat there and listened to my tape alone."

"Do you mean to say that you've done this sort of thing three times before . . . and nobody came?"

"Yes!"

"What are you, some kind of masochist? Why would you bother trying to promote something that nobody is interested in?"

Kathy stopped walking right there and put her hands on her hips as she said, "The only reason most people aren't interested in the message is because they haven't heard it yet. I figure that if I can offer the tapes enough times, I will eventually attract those who are ready for mystical Truth. And remember, Mister-Great-Spiritual-Light-of-the-Western -World, I did manage to flush you out of the bushes, didn't I?"

This girl certainly does have a way with words, I thought. Maybe she should just give speeches herself instead of playing tapes. . . . Tapes. . . ? Does she have more than just this one recorded lecture?

"Kathy, you mentioned that you want to offer your tapes to the world. . . . You said 'tapes' with an 's'. That's plural, meaning more than one?"

"Right! I have several tapes."

"Where did you get those?"

"The same way . . . in the mail. . . . They just come to me every few months."

"And you really don't know where they're coming from?"

"No! Although I often think that Mr. Hunt has something to do with it. He did tell me that I would continue to be taught."

"When did he tell you that? Did you see Mr. Hunt after our episode with him in the park?"

"Yes! Oh, and come to think of it, when I met him, he also told me that someday I'd be with you again. That's why I'm rather surprised that it took me so long to recognize you when you came into the room tonight."

For a fleeting moment, I felt a pang of jealousy toward Kathy. How did she get a second audience with Mr. Hunt? I had never had a repeat encounter with my spiritual teachers. I then asked, "When did you see Mr. Hunt for the second time?"

"It was on the day after my father had told us that we'd be moving to Cincinnati. I cried myself to sleep the night he gave us that news. The next day was Saturday, and I was feeling very despondent, so I climbed on my bicycle and rode around St. Louis to all of my favorite places. My most favorite place of all was that park where Pam and you and I had been together. As I rode near the area where we had had our conversation, I unexpectedly noticed Mr. Hunt sitting on a park bench. I stopped my bike rather abruptly in front of him. When he saw me, he smiled warmly and said: 'Good morning, Kathy! It's nice to see you again.'

"I wondered how he remembered my name. Yet it seemed as though he had been sitting there specifically waiting just for me. Anyway, we got into a long discussion on spiritual Truth. But then as he became aware of my obvious depression, he asked what was troubling me. I told him that I felt so badly about moving away from all of my friends. He said that our real friends are those people who are of our own spiritual household, and he pointed out that these friends can never be lost. Then he told me that you and Pam were the only true friends that I had at that time.... And that's when he also told me that I would meet you again someday because, according to his words: 'we share a common spiritual destiny.'"

"We share a common spiritual destiny?" What did he mean by that statement? And how could he have known such a thing so many years ago. Nevertheless, after hearing that prophecy, I no longer felt jealous of Kathy, but rather I was extremely grateful that she had had this second encounter with Mr. Hunt.

Chapter Ten

I walked Kathy back to her dormitory that evening. Her room was located on the opposite end of the campus from mine. Maybe that was why we never had crossed paths during her almost two years at the university. But now that she had come back into my life, I made a silent vow that it would take nothing less than a congressional resolution or a presidential decree to get her away from me again.

On the two days following the taped lecture meeting, both Kathy and I had a number of previous commitments, so we agreed not to see each other until the following Friday evening when we would go out to dinner.

Being extremely anxious to see her by that time, I arrived at Kathy's dormitory ten minutes before our scheduled date. She invited me into her room and introduced me to her roommate—an attractive girl named Lisa. After a few slightly awkward moments, which were precipitated by my incessant shyness, the girls offered me a seat on the only available guest chair in their room. Then the three of us engaged in some irrelevant small talk for about five minutes until Lisa excused herself and went out for the evening. Just as Lisa was leaving, I glanced up at the bookshelf located directly above Kathy's desk. The shelf was filled with college textbooks and other manuscripts. Leaning against the wall on the far right side of the shelf, however, was a small black leather book. I rose from my chair and removed the book from the shelf. While nonchalantly scanning the cover, I was startled to see the words: "THE GOSPEL According to 'I AM'".

"Kathy!" I asked. "Have you ever read this book?"

"Oh, that? Sure! I read it all the time."

"Where did you buy it?"

"Are you certain that you really want to know?"

"Yes!"

"I didn't buy it!"

"Then where did you get it? No . . . wait . . . let me guess. It came in the mail in a plain brown wrapper . . . and you didn't order it . . . and you have no idea where it came from! Right?"

"Right! Now you're catching on, Eric!"

Maybe Kathy and I would never have an opportunity to share the "common spiritual destiny" that Mr. Hunt had promised, but we certainly had already shared a rather mysterious "spiritual past."

I placed the book back on its shelf and we left her room, walking several blocks to a small Italian restaurant located just east of the campus. I was anticipating a most enjoyable evening, as the two of us would have a chance to become reacquainted with each other. After we were seated at our table, I asked the question:

"Kathy, do you have any idea of the identity of the lecturer on your tapes?"

"No, do you?"

"Yes! I think it's Shimahn!"

With a very serious frown on her face, she asked, "What's a Shimahn?"

"Kathy! Don't you remember my story about Old Jerusalem?"

"Yes, I remember your story! That was supposed to be a joke, Eric. Where's your sense of humor? I just wanted to remind you of our old friend, 'Doubting Thomas'."

"Oh, good old Thomas! I wonder whatever became of him?"

"Seriously, Eric, do you really think the voice on the tapes is Shimahn?"

"Yes! But I wonder who's been sending them to you. When you met with Mr. Hunt that second time, didn't you ask him any questions?"

"What kind of questions?"

"Questions like: What's this mystical stuff all about? And how did he just happen to be sitting on that park bench the day us kids were talking on the grass? And how did he know me when he walked up to us? He said he knew Shimahn. What's their relationship? Is Mr. Hunt one of Shimahn's agents? And how did he just happen to be sitting there that day when you were so depressed and needed help? What is he, some kind of guardian angel?"

"I'm beginning to wonder about you, Kathy. How could you be granted a second audience with an enlightened master like Mr. Hunt and then not ask him any questions?"

"I'm sorry, Eric! I guess I was pretty depressed that day, and I just didn't think of asking him anything. And besides, all of my spiritual adventures happened after we moved to Cincinnati."

"What do you mean, 'spiritual adventures?' Aside from getting a few unexplained books and tapes in the mail, whatever happened to you?"

After I had made that rather conceited statement, Kathy began mockingly bowing toward me as she sarcastically said: "Please forgive me, O-Great-Wise-One-from-Jerusalem. I almost forgot that you have been granted the sole and exclusive right to sit at the feet of Tibetan masters. Most of the rest of us mortals consider ourselves pretty fortunate if we merely receive an occasional book or tape in the mail!"

Realizing that I deserved that stinging reprimand, I quickly apologized for acting so arrogant. I then asked Kathy what she meant when she spoke about having some spiritual adventures after moving to Cincinnati.

"You know, I never have told anyone about this, Eric, but I did have a most unique experience during my final year of high school." She glanced around the dining room for a moment and then said: "In the spring of that year, my parents and I had taken a trip to New Orleans to see the Mardi Gras celebration. On the day of the big parade, Mom and Dad wanted to spend the afternoon relaxing in our room, to rest up for the evening's festivities; so I decided to take a walk in the area around our hotel in the French Quarter. After browsing through a number of interesting souvenir and antique shops, I came upon an ornately carved door which offered entrance to a quaint little store whose façade was decorated in a unique nautical theme. As I approached the building, I noticed a small hand-carved wooden sign just above the door. The sign read:

At that point in her discourse, I almost swallowed my tongue. But before I could interrupt her, Kathy continued:
"'Fishermen's Realm', I thought, what an interesting name. I was unable to see into the shop because of the very dark stained-glass windows. But being thoroughly intrigued by what I might find inside, I quickly opened the door. As I entered, I was quite surprised by what I saw. It was an intimate little shop in which a few strange-looking people were sitting in meditation, and there were several Arabs lurking in the dark corners. In a little room off to the side, I even saw a Hindu snake charmer plying his trade. In addition, the entire building was filled with smoke and was imbued with the aroma of burning incense."

As Kathy mentioned the word "incense", I could hardly keep from exploding. I rudely interrupted her: "That never happened! You just made up that story, didn't you?"

Looking very insulted by my rash insinuation, she snapped: "Here we go again! The enlightened mystic, who consorts with the wise men in Israel, knows all and sees all! What kind of remark was that, Eric? You tell me something weird like you have sat at the table where Jesus and his disciples had their last supper, and then you don't believe my simple little story?"

Once again she had me on the defensive. "I'm sorry, Kathy! I didn't mean to insult you, but your story sounded utterly fantastic to me. You see, I had a similar experience in San Francisco a few years ago. When my mother and I were visiting Fisherman's Wharf, I discovered a little shop that looked just like yours—at least from the outside. It had the same hand-carved wooden sign above the door, and the store's name was 'Fishermen's Realm'. Then just before I opened the door, I tried to visualize what the interior would look like. In my mind I saw everything that you just described: the people in meditation, the Arabs in the corners, the snake charmer . . . even the burning incense."

"That's incredible, Eric!"

"I know! But even more amazing is the fact that I merely had conjured up that whole scene in my mind. When I opened the door, my shop didn't look anything like that. It was a brightly-lit showroom full of all kinds of books, and souvenirs and real people."

Kathy quietly stared at me for a few seconds and then said, "Maybe there's a Fishermen's Realm store in every major city. Maybe it's a franchise, like McDonald's."

I didn't even bother replying to that comment. Instead, I said, "Tell me more about your little nautical shop in New Orleans."

Reflecting back on the episode, Kathy once again mysteriously looked around the dining room to assure herself that no one was listening. Then she began speaking softly:

"Just after I entered the shop, the group that had been meditating ended their session and quietly started dispersing. They were a strange-looking lot, but I suppose part of the reason for that was the fact that several of them were already wearing their Mardi Gras costumes.

"I didn't want to appear to be staring at them, so I began browsing through some of the nautical antiques and artifacts. From one of the tables near the center of the room, I picked up a very old compass. I was quietly studying the instrument when suddenly I was startled by a woman's screechy voice coming from over my shoulder.

"'That's a very special piece you're lookin' at there, dearie!'

"I almost dropped the compass when I heard her voice. I wasn't aware that anyone had been standing there behind me. Turning around to face her, I recalled that, when I had first entered the store, this woman was sitting on a bench in one of the corners, talking to a man who was dressed like an Arab. She, herself, was wearing a Moslem veil. At first, I couldn't tell if these people really were Arabs, or if they merely were attired in Mardi Gras costumes. Then I realized that this strange-looking lady couldn't be a Moslem, because she had bright yellow hair that obviously had been bleached that color. In addition, her hair was pulled back tightly in a bun—a style of hairdo that was popular back in the forties.

"I then said, 'I'm sorry! I'm just browsing,' as I placed the compass back on the table.

"'That one was used by Old Blackbeard hisself,' she said.

"I really didn't believe that assertion, but I tried not to let my feelings show, as I slowly walked away from her.

"'You don't believe that that's Blackbeard's compass, do ya?' she asked, as she closely followed me to the next table.

"'I'm sorry, I really don't have any opinion about that. If you say it's Blackbeard's compass, then I believe you,' I answered, as I unconsciously picked up a piece of fishing net from the next table.

"Though I couldn't see her mouth because of the veil she was wearing, her eyes lit up indicating that she was pleased by my reply. She then said, 'That fishing net was used by Simon Peter.'

"I silently stared into her eyes as she said, 'You know, Peter, the Big Fisherman . . . he was one of Jesus' disciples.'

"'Oh!' was all I could say.

"'You don't believe me again, do ya?' she asked. 'Really . . . when they made that big catch that day when Jesus told them to cast their nets on the right side of the boat. . . . This is a piece of Peter's net.'

"Right about that time, I was beginning to squirm a little. My hands were starting to sweat, and I was wishing that this crazy lady would just go away and leave me alone. Before I could do anything to extricate myself from the situation, the woman who had been conducting the meditation group approached us. Placing her left hand on the veiled lady's shoulder, she said:

"'Geraldine, are you bothering this young lady with your tall tales again?'

"I breathed a sigh of relief as the second woman then said, 'Don't mind Geri. She's perfectly harmless, but she does add a bit of color to the store, don't you think?'

"I didn't think the store needed much more color. The lady with the yellow hair curtsied toward me and then walked away, joining one of the Arabs in the corner.

"The second woman, who spoke with a slight French accent, then said, 'I hope Geraldine didn't make you feel too uncomfortable. As soon as I saw her heading in your direction, I realized that I should come over to help you out. But our little meditation group was just breaking up, and I had to give them their next assignments.'"

At that point, I interrupted Kathy by asking her to describe this lady.

"You really would have liked her, Eric. She obviously was imbued with the Spirit. Her hair was almost completely white, and yet she projected a youthful exuberance that belied her age. But what impressed me most of all was the feeling of love that permeated her being. She was the most 'loving' person I have ever met."

Jokingly, I asked, "Was she even more 'loving' than me?"

Kathy giggled, and said, "Yes, Eric, she was even more 'loving' than you," as she softly squeezed my hand.

I then asked, "What was the lady's name?"

Kathy replied, "She told me that her name was Jeanne Baptiste . . . and she wanted me to call her 'Jeanne' . . . but let me continue my story. . . . As the strange lady with the yellow hair was walking away from us, I asked Jeanne:

"'Doesn't it hurt the shop's reputation to have that kind of person loitering here and bothering the customers? Why does the owner allow it?'

"Jeanne answered, 'Geraldine *is* the owner of the shop!'

"I stared at Jeanne with a bewildered frown on my face. She smiled and said:

"'Don't be alarmed by the strange costumes you're seeing in the shop today. Aside from Geri, it's a very normal group of people. They're all just getting ready for the big Mardi Gras celebration tonight.'

"I then asked, 'But the people who were meditating with you. . . ? What kind of teaching are you following?'

"Jeanne replied, 'Like yourself, we're all students of Primitive Christian Mysticism.'"

Once again, I interrupted Kathy. "So that's where you found that name for the teaching! I've been wanting to talk to you about that. . . . But what did Jeanne mean when she said: 'Like yourself?' How could she know that you were interested in spiritual Truth?"

"I wondered about that too, Eric. As you might suspect, I was rather startled by Jeanne's remark. When I asked her for an explanation, she replied:

"'Don't be alarmed, Kathy. It's a very natural thing for those of us on the path to recognize each other. We are of the same spiritual household and, more than likely, have shared many experiences in past lifetimes.'

"At that point in our conversation, Jeanne began walking toward the small side room where the snake charmer had been sitting earlier. When I inquired about him, Jeanne laughed as she said:

"'Oh, that was Harry Collingsworth. He's a local actor who was merely rehearsing for a TV commercial that they're going to film tomorrow. He didn't actually have a snake in the basket.'

"I was quite relieved to hear that. As we entered the room, Jeanne invited me to sit next to her on a small couch. She continued our conversation by saying:

"'You know, Kathy, there is only one basic Truth . . . and that Truth reveals that God is all that exists. Therefore, each one of us can partake of all the wisdom and knowledge that already are established in Divine Consciousness. As we continue to spend time in meditation and communion, we gradually develop a higher awareness of ultimate reality. Through this expanded spiritual state of consciousness, we discover faculties of perception that, previously, we never knew existed. And it was through these faculties that I was able to recognize your inherent receptivity to Truth and your highly developed Soul sense.'

"After she had made that statement, Jeanne and I just sat quietly for a few moments. As you would expect, I was rather curious about her background. I wondered if she had ever met Mr. Hunt. Maybe both of them were students of the same mystical philosophy.

"I broke the silence by asking: 'Jeanne, do you know a man named Mr. Hunt? I think he lives in St. Louis.'

"'I'm sorry, Kathy, but I don't believe that he and I have ever crossed paths in this incarnation.'

"I replied, 'Mr. Hunt was the man who introduced me to mysticism. In fact, it was with him that I had my initial experience in meditation. Evidently, he had quite a solid understanding of spiritual principles. He also seemed to have some highly developed Soul faculties, because he made several comments about my future. And, at one point in our discussion, he even told me that I had a very unique spiritual destiny.'

"'That's most interesting, Kathy. I always enjoy learning about others on the path. It's very possible that your Mr. Hunt and I share a common spiritual heritage. And as for your future, I, too, feel that you have an important work ahead of you.'

"I then asked Jeanne, 'What work could I possibly do? I don't have any spiritual training. In fact, I hardly ever even go to church.'

"She answered, 'It's not important if we are on the inside or the outside of a church. The spiritual consciousness of mankind can be lifted up only when some individual recognizes the divinity of his own being and then lives his life as the 'light of the world.'

"'As you probably know, throughout recorded history, there have been any number of men and women who have achieved illumination—an absolute recognition of their true identity. Quite often, these enlightened beings have attracted followers who were of like mind and were receptive to the message. In most cases, however, the teaching faded away soon after the death of the original messenger. But in a few instances, the illumined revelators founded organized religious movements. Then after the founder's passing, the students and followers tried to perpetuate the teaching by carrying on the work. But more often than not, as time passed, many of these organized movements lost sight of the original teacher's message and mission, and, consequently, the great light of Truth, once again, was extinguished.'

"Jeanne continued: 'While there have been many different approaches to Truth, almost without exception, all absolute teachings are based on the fundamental premise that *God is All*. When that fact is firmly established in consciousness, the rest of the principles will follow logically. These, in turn, lead us to a realization that conscious union with God must be our ultimate goal. And when you think about it, wasn't that what Jesus was doing? He was in constant communion with God. He lived in a perpetual state of mystical union with his Source. I personally believe that that was the real purpose of Jesus' mission here on earth. He gave us a pure form of Primitive Christian Mysticism.'

"Jeanne saw that I was agreeing with her, so she just kept right on talking: 'Frankly, it is not important if a spiritual revelator creates a formal organization or if he does not. The true significance of any teacher's work is determined, first, by the measure of spiritual illumination that he achieves and, then, by the degree to which he can uplift the consciousness of his student body.

"'And that, Kathy, is what makes this present time so exciting. We are approaching a new era in spiritual unfoldment. The foundational teachings of Christ Jesus, coupled with the work of other illumined mystics who have followed him, have raised the consciousness of mankind to a point where great numbers of people will soon be ready to accept absolute Truth . . . and you will have an important role to play in this work. . . .'

"Jeanne closed her eyes and, after a few seconds of silence, said, 'Kathy, it has been revealed to me that you have been chosen to make the preparations for the sacred ministry of a highly enlightened master. As John the Baptist set the stage for Christ Jesus, so will you introduce this great teacher of spiritual wisdom. . . .'"

Continuing her story, Kathy then said: "Needless to say, I was rather astonished by that prophecy. After pondering what she had just told me, I touched Jeanne's hand and asked: 'But why me. . . ? I don't know any enlightened masters, except possibly for Mr. Hunt; and I wouldn't even know where to find him. Who is this great teacher that you spoke about? What is his name?'

"With her eyes still closed, Jeanne replied, 'His identity has not been revealed to me, Kathy. I only know that after you have been in his presence, you will recognize him as a spiritually enlightened soul. This master received his mystical initiation several lifetimes ago and, since that time, has continued to grow in wisdom and stature.'"

Looking softly into my eyes, Kathy then said: "After that statement, Jeanne stopped speaking. She continued to sit with her eyes closed, and almost immediately I felt a great desire to join her in meditation. As we sat there in silence, I very quickly achieved an overwhelming but joyous awareness of mystical union with the Divine Presence. It was similar to the sensation I had experienced that day in the park with Pam and you and Mr. Hunt."

I was extremely impressed by Kathy's depiction of her episode in New Orleans. At that point I asked her, "Did Jeanne say any more about the teacher that you're supposed to meet some day?"

"No, Eric. After we concluded our meditation, she placed her hands on my shoulders and said, 'Go in peace, Dear One. Remember to continue working with the spiritual principles. And most important of all: Follow your destiny!'

"Then I left the shop and pondered what I had just heard as I leisurely walked back to our hotel to join my parents for an early dinner."

I then asked, "Is that why you've been playing your tapes for the general public? Do you feel that the teacher on the recordings might be the new Messiah that you're supposed to introduce?"

Kathy replied, "I really don't know, Eric. He is the closest thing to a spiritual master that I have come across. And I certainly haven't met any other likely candidates recently."

Since we had finished dinner by that time, I paid the waitress, and Kathy and I quietly left the restaurant. While the two of us had been in steady conversation for most of the evening, we suddenly seemed to share a mutual desire for silence as we savored the warm spring air on our very pleasant walk back to her dormitory. That Friday evening date was only the first of many such occasions. Apparently we were extremely attracted to each other, because we made a point of spending some time together—even if only for a short while—during every one of the remaining days of that school year.

Chapter Eleven

As Kathy and I continued to spend most of our free time together, it became increasingly evident to me that I could no longer consider living the rest of my life without her at my side. But even though she seemed to share my feelings, and we, more or less, had begun to take each other for granted, I was becoming a little concerned about Jeanne Baptiste's prediction that, someday, Kathy would be the forerunner of an eminent teacher of spiritual wisdom. I certainly wouldn't want her to devote all her future time to travelling around the world, sitting at the feet of some unknown guru.

Then approximately three weeks before the end of our school year, I received a most interesting announcement in the mail. The announcement told of a new government-subsidized program that made it possible for qualifying college juniors and seniors to participate in a student foreign-exchange plan. For me, the most intriguing aspect of the program was the fact that American students would be allowed to spend up to sixteen weeks in India, receiving full college credits for their studies there. And, after all, once you were in India, wouldn't it be just a hop, skip and jump to get into Tibet. . . ?

I hadn't mentioned anything to Kathy about the foreign-exchange program until the weekend before our final exams. To celebrate the end of our school year, the two of us had decided to take a break from our studies by having one last dinner at our favorite Italian restaurant.

As we were sitting in the dining room on that Saturday evening, after we had finished our salads and were waiting for our entrees, I handed Kathy the announcement which described the trip to India.

She studied the paper for a moment and then said, "It sounds like it could be an interesting experience, Eric. But surely you're not thinking about going, are you?"

"I don't know, Kathy. I have given it some serious consideration, and the more I think about it, the stronger my desire becomes. As you know, India is right next to Tibet. . . ."

"Oh, Eric, I know how much Shimahn meant to you. But even if you could locate him, he'd be almost one hundred years old now—that is, if he's still alive."

"Of course he's still alive, Kathy! How could you even think such a thought? I guarantee that when we find him, you'll agree that he looks like he's only about forty."

"What do you mean, 'we', Eric? You certainly don't expect me to go with you, do you?"

"Why not? I've always wanted you to meet Shimahn."

"But you have no idea where he is! Where could you even begin looking? And what do you expect me to do, climb up and down the snow-covered peaks of the Himalayan Mountains with you?"

"No, Kathy," I answered. "It wouldn't be anything as far-fetched as that. I thought I might visit Pam in St. Louis this summer. Then while I'm there, maybe I could track down Mr. Hunt, and he'd be able to tell me how to find Shimahn."

"But, Eric, even if you did get Shimahn's address, I couldn't just go off to the Far East with you as your travelling companion. My parents would never allow that."

After Kathy made that comment, I couldn't resist taking the opportunity to say: "Okay, I confess! You've finally caught on to my motives! All this while you thought that I was interested in your mind and your highly developed mystical capacities. But now you know the truth.... I've really been after your fabulous body!"

As I finished that statement, Kathy's big brown eyes opened even wider than I had ever seen them before. I then gently reached across the table and, taking her hands in mine, I said:

"You realize that I was only joking, don't you? Gosh, Honey, I wouldn't expect you to just run off with me, looking like some type of 'kept woman.' I assumed that we'd get married first and then take the trip to India."

For a brief interval, it appeared that Kathy was about to lose her normally cool and unruffled equanimity as her cheeks became flushed and she smiled sheepishly. But very quickly regaining her composure, she asked:

"When did that word become a part of your vocabulary? Was that actually a proposal of marriage, or were you just using one of those trial closes that they teach us about in marketing class?"

Looking directly at her, I said, "I'm very serious, Kathy. You know how much I love you, and I really do want to marry you."

At that moment, I noticed a slight glistening in her eyes as she said, "Oh, Eric, are you sure? You know, we really haven't known each other for all that long a time."

I answered, "You certainly don't believe that, do you? Don't you realize that you are my Soulmate? Our relationship was established several lifetimes ago."

"Gee whiz, Eric! If you put it that way, how can I refuse?"

"You can't," I replied. "And aside from that, who else would ever want to get involved with someone as weird as either one of us?"

By the time we had finished our desserts, Kathy had accepted my proposal of marriage. But she didn't want our wedding plans to be rushed, or to be conditional on our making the trip to India. So I agreed to not even think about the foreign-exchange program again until we had enjoyed a few relaxing weeks of our summer vacation.

After completing our exams and wrapping up the loose ends of the school year, Kathy and I decided to be apart for awhile as we went back to our respective homes to break the news of our engagement to our parents. Not unexpectedly, both of our families were quite surprised at the glad tidings, because neither of us had given them any previous indication that we were so emotionally involved with anyone. After all, we had been dating each other for less than two months, and even though Kathy and I were aware of our background, how could we possibly tell them that she and I probably have been together for the past six or seven hundred years?

During the fourth week of June, I drove to Cincinnati to meet Kathy's parents. Up to that time, she and I had either phoned or written to one another on every single day since we had left Purdue University.

Evidently Kathy had done a good selling job on her parents, because they were extremely pleasant to me. And once the initial shock of her announcement had subsided, they appeared to have resigned themselves to graciously "losing" their only daughter. In fact, never before had I met two complete strangers—except for Shimahn and Nehemiah—with whom I could so quickly feel at ease. And just one glimpse of her mother revealed the source of Kathy's physical beauty. The two of them could almost have passed for sisters.

After I had spent four days with Kathy's family, she rode back to Chicago with me so that my parents would have their opportunity to meet her. As with my reception in Cincinnati, Kathy was very warmly received and accepted by my parents. So now that we had been given the unconditional blessings of both families, I felt that it was time for us to begin making some more specific plans. I still had that itch in my feet to run off to India.

On the third evening of our stay in Chicago, I once again broached the subject to Kathy. Not wanting to alarm her, I rather meekly began talking about the foreign-exchange program.

Sensing my obvious disconcertion, Kathy laughed softly and then said, "Oh, Eric, you don't have to act so coy about it. I won't be angry with you if we talk about your trip to 'Never-Never Land'. Believe it or not, I have given it quite a bit of thought myself."

"You have?" I asked.

"Yes, Eric! But I don't think it would be worth going to India unless we could be certain that we could get into Tibet. And even more important, we definitely should know that we have a chance of finding Shimahn when we get there."

"What do you mean, 'we', Kathy? what makes you think that I would want to take you along? I'd be missing my opportunities with all those exotic Far Eastern women."

"Ha! Ha!" was all she said, as she continued giving me her thoughts on the subject: "I think your original idea of going to St. Louis to try to find Mr. Hunt was a good one, and I certainly would like to go back there again. I haven't communicated with your cousin Pam in more than six years. We wrote to each other a few times after I moved away, but then we just seemed to fall out of touch. . . . And I'll bet Pam will really be excited to hear that the two of us have met again and are getting married."

"Sounds good to me, Kathy. You know, earlier in the year, my mother had talked about going to St. Louis for the July 4th holiday. Maybe we all could go together and stay at my Uncle Art's house for a few days."

My parents were quite receptive to the idea, so my father made arrangements for the four of us to fly to St. Louis on the following weekend.

Overjoyed at hearing the news about her old friend and me, Pamela was waiting for us at the airport. As we disembarked from the plane, she and Kathy immediately embraced each other in a tearful, but joyous, reunion.

That evening, Pam, Kathy and I sat on my uncle's screened-in back porch until two a.m., as we brought each other up to date on our personal activities over the last seven years. Pam listened very intently as Kathy told us about her mystical adventure in New Orleans. When Kathy came to the prediction that, someday, she would introduce an illumined spiritual teacher, Pam seemed to want to say something, but then she shook her head as though, suddenly, she was at a loss for words.

When I brought up the subject of the trip to India, all three of us agreed that we should try to locate Mr. Hunt. Our first inclination was to look in the white pages of the Greater St. Louis telephone directory. As might be expected, there were more than one-hundred-thirty people named "Hunt", and we didn't even know our enlightened master's first name. We began joking about how ridiculous it would be to randomly begin calling names in the phone book, especially at one o'clock in the morning.

Pam suddenly started giggling uncontrollably. Then she went into a comic routine in which she dialed a number on an imaginary telephone. Speaking with a very sultry voice, she then said:

"Hello, M'am! Is Mr. Hunt there. . . ? He's not. . . ? Oh, well, I wonder if you can tell me if he's a mystical guru who approaches young children in parks and then talks to them about God. . . ? How old am I, you ask. . . ? Oh, I'm twenty years old now, but I was only thirteen when your husband first approached me . . . CLICK. . . ! Oh, I guess she just hung up!"

By the time Pam had finished her routine, Kathy and I were practically rolling on the floor. Pam had made her point, so we ruled out the possibility of trying to find him by using the telephone.

Then just before the three of us decided to retire for the evening, Kathy suggested that, since the next day would be Friday, maybe we should all go to the park where we had had our initial encounter with Mr. Hunt. Pam and I agreed.

At ten-thirty the next morning, my cousin, my fiancee and I took the short but pleasant walk to our by now notorious park. We stayed in the area for more than five and a half hours, even eating lunch at a small pavilion near the park's lagoon, but our hoped-for meeting with our spiritual master never took place. Nonetheless, we probably would have stayed even longer, but slightly after four p.m. a light drizzle began to fall and, reluctantly, we decided to return to Pam's house.

That evening, after the three of us had spent some more time catching up on old times, Kathy made an interesting comment:

"You know, kids, either we all have been fooled, and these alleged spiritual principles are somebody's idea of a bad joke, or else there really is some divine purpose in our lives. Here, Eric wants to see Shimahn again; we all want to see Mr. Hunt again; and someday—hopefully in the not-too-distant future—I'm supposed to be led to the new Messiah, so I can beat a path for him. . . . What I'm trying to say is: I think the three of us should have a meditation right now!"

I replied, "you're right, Kathy! That's a good idea!"

Pam said, "I agree. . . ! Why don't you lead us in a meditation, Eric?"

Kathy stole a quick glance at Pam, and then, looking back at me, she said, "Why not. . . ? Eric. . . ?"

We all closed our eyes and sat silently for a few minutes. Then I began to speak . . . or shall I say, a voice spoke through me: "There is only one infinite Consciousness. Each one of us is an individualized expression of that One. Therefore, each one of us includes within ourself all the wisdom, all the knowledge, all the power of God. Our birthright demands that we be spiritually fulfilled. Those people who are necessary to our progress on the path must appear at the proper time and in the proper place. We don't know our destiny. We don't seek any specific role to play. We are not here to outline our personal desires. But we are willing to become an empty vessel—a virtual transparency through which the will of the Father can be fulfilled."

At that point, the words stopped coming, and the three of us sat in silence for several minutes. When we finished the meditation, Pam said, "Boy, that was super, Eric!" Looking at Kathy, she then said, "Wasn't he great?"

Kathy replied, "Yeah. . . ? He was fantastic!" as she stared at me with an astonished look on her face. For just a fleeting moment, I sensed a feeling in Kathy that she truly had never known me before and was just seeing me for the first time.

Then the two girls came up to me and each kissed me on the cheek. I pulled Kathy back into my arms, however, as I said: "Hey! Just a minute! It's all right for my cousin to kiss me like that, but not my fiancee." She then gave me a more appropriate kiss on the lips, and the two of them said, "Good night, Eric," as they retired to the room that they shared. I was already in my "bedroom" since I had been nominated to sleep on the back porch for the duration of our visit.

As I lay on the couch, I pondered the words that I had spoken in the meditation—especially the phrase: "Those people who are necessary to our progress on the path must appear at the proper time and in the proper place."

Though I wanted to see Mr. Hunt again, I realized that I couldn't will something to happen by merely using some untapped power of my mind. All the spiritual principles that I had learned up to that time indicated that the human mind is not a power but rather is an instrument for our use—an instrument through which we can become aware of spiritual Truth. But, ultimately, this human-sense-of-mind must surrender itself and must achieve a mystical union with the Divine Consciousness. Then, in that moment of God-realization, we witness the "immaculate conception" as the Christ of God is awakened in us. This Christ then lives our life and goes before us to "make the crooked places straight."

When we function as a pure state of Christ-consciousness, all the people, all the circumstances, all the conditions necessary for our spiritual fulfillment must appear in our experience.

At that point in my meditation, my mind became still, and I accepted that divine Truth as the Word of God. "Resting in that Word," I achieved the transcendental sense of oneness with God that, by then, was becoming a fairly regular occurrence for me.

The next morning was a warm, sunny day, and Pam, Kathy and I were all out of bed very early. However, we decided to stay around the house for most of the morning. Then shortly after noon, and after eating a light lunch, the three of us walked back to the park for one final attempt at meeting Mr. Hunt.

After entering the park, we headed directly for the area where we had had our encounter seven years earlier. From that vantage point, we looked around at the people sitting on the nearby benches, but we saw no familiar faces.

Then, pointing a finger to my right, I said, "Say, girls, why don't we just sit down on that sunny patch of grass over there?"

"I like that idea," Pamela said, as she started walking in that direction. Following Pam's lead, the two of us joined her, and we all casually sat down on the grass.

Kathy glanced around the area one last time and then suggested: "What would you think of meditating here for a little while?"

Pam and I agreed, so we all closed our eyes and sat quietly as the midday sun baked down upon us.

After several peaceful minutes, my cousin's voice broke the silence: "Hey, kids, guess who's here?"

Kathy and I opened our eyes simultaneously as we beheld the smiling but still-dignified face of Mr. Hunt looking down at us. His hair appeared to be a little grayer and a little thinner on top, but otherwise he looked exactly as he did seven years before. In fact, he still was wearing the same three-piece gray, pin-striped suit adorned with the gold pocket watch.

Sitting down on the grass with us, Mr. Hunt said, "Good afternoon, young people. It's so nice to see all of you again."

Pam then said, "What are you, some kind of magic genie? The last time I closed my eyes in this park, you disappeared. Now I close my eyes again, and you materialize out of nowhere."

Kathy spoke up: "Pamela, how can you say such a thing? After all, we did want to meet Mr. Hunt again, and now he's finally here with us."

Pam replied, "I didn't mean any offence, Mr. Hunt. It's just that both Kathy and Eric have had a lot more experience with these adventures in mysticism. This spooky stuff is all a little new for me."

"That's all right, Pam, I understand," he said. This spiritually illumined man then looked at each of us and asked, "How may I be of help to you at this time?"

I answered, "We have all kinds of questions for you. But first of all—and you probably already know this—Kathy and I are going to be married."

"That's wonderful," he said. "Congratulations!"

I then demanded: "Now before we say another word, and before you disappear again, I'd like to know your first name, and I want your telephone number!"

"I'm sorry, Eric! I believe I did overlook those formalities at our last meeting. Here is my card. . . ."

He reached into his pocket and pulled out a very plain gray business card on which were listed his name and telephone number. I had the feeling that if I would have asked instead for his address and date of birth, he simply would have reached into his pocket and pulled out a card with that information on it.

Looking at the card, I rather mockingly shouted: "Jeremy Hunt. . . ? Gee, girls, that would have been an easy one to find in the phone book!"

He quickly corrected me: "Oh, you wouldn't have found me in the book. That number on the card is unpublished."

"Naturally!" I thought. I wondered if the number on the card was really a working telephone. Anyway, I didn't think they had telephones in heaven, or wherever this strange little man had been spending his time for the last seven years.

I then said, "Mr. Hunt, when we first met you in this park, you told me that you knew Shimahn. Well, Kathy and I may have an opportunity to travel to Tibet next spring, and we'd like to visit with him."

Kathy interjected, "Does Shimahn still live in Tibet? Is he still teaching Truth?"

Our diminutive friend smiled, as he so often did before answering our questions. Then, sounding as though he had discerned the real question that she was asking, he said, "Yes, Kathy! Shimahn is still with us on this plane of existence. As a matter of fact, he has been doing a good deal of teaching in his native land and throughout Asia Minor."

I then asked, "Mr. Hunt, can you give us directions on how to locate Shimahn?"

"I can," he said, "but I question why you feel the need to see him again."

"Because he is my teacher!" I replied somewhat indignantly. "It was Shimahn who introduced me to Truth. It was because of him that I had my first mystical experience. I have wanted to see him again ever since he and Nehemiah left me in Jerusalem. Oh . . . and how about my old friend Nehemiah? What is he doing these days?"

Mr. Hunt answered, "Evidently you haven't been told, Eric, but Nehemiah made his transition a little over two years ago."

Pam queried, "Made his transition. . . ? Are you telling us that he's dead?"

"We don't think of it in those terms, Pam," he replied. "Death would imply an end to life . . . but we know that there is only one Life, and that Life is immortal and eternal. Therefore, after our work on this plane is finished, it is only natural that we move on to our next experience. If we are on an ascending scale of spiritual unfoldment, we will continue functioning, but at a higher level of awareness."

Those words sounded fairly logical, but nonetheless I was saddened to hear of Nehemiah's passing. I then asked, "Mr. Hunt, I still question why someone as spiritually illumined as Nehemiah had to die like any other mortal. Was he ill? Couldn't Shimahn have healed him?"

"Eric, you know the answers to those questions!" he retorted. "As I told you, Nehemiah isn't dead! He is merely functioning at a higher level of consciousness. His work here was finished. He was being hampered by the built-in limitations of his physical body. I give you my word . . . right this very moment, Nehemiah is 'about his Father's business.'"

Kathy then spoke up: "Mr. Hunt, I have a question. . . . A few years ago, a seemingly enlightened lady told me that I was destined to pave the way for a highly developed teacher of spiritual wisdom. Do you know anything about that?"

"Yes, Kathy," he answered. "Your work will begin soon."

"But I don't know any illumined masters at this time. When will I meet him? Where will I find him?"

He smiled and said, "You already have!"

"I have?" she questioned.

Kathy glanced at me and shrugged her shoulders. Mr. Hunt then said, "You really don't know, do you?" as he momentarily studied each one of us. When he looked at Pamela, their expressions seemed to indicate that the two of them shared some special awareness that Kathy and I weren't perceiving.

With an enthusiastic grin, Pam then said, "Eric's the one, isn't he?"

Mr. Hunt's face lit up as I blurted out, "Eric's the one what?"

"You're the new spiritual teacher," Pam replied. "I realized it the other evening on our back porch when Kathy told us about Jeanne Baptiste's prediction."

At that moment, Kathy's face rapidly progressed through a whole series of changing expressions. At first, she appeared somewhat stunned and, then, rather astonished. Next, I thought I noticed an aura of pride surrounding her as she shyly smiled at me. But then, as the full realization of what had just been said came through to Kathy, she nodded her head in agreement: "Of course, Eric, you're the one!" she said.

Needless to say, I was quite shocked by what I was hearing. "Why me?" I asked. "I don't desire any such thing. And I certainly don't deserve it!"

"But, Eric," Kathy said, "just consider your background! Do you think it was merely an accident that you met Shimahn and Nehemiah in Old Jerusalem?"

Then Pam interjected: "And just think about this, Eric. . . . You haven't experienced just one isolated encounter with a spiritually illumined person. . . . You've had several of those. And I'm quite certain that even Kathy and I have been led to mystical Truth as a direct result of our being in your presence. And. . . ."

I interrupted her: "Come on, Pam! Knock it off! Those were just coincidences!"

Hoping to find someone who would agree with me, I pleadingly looked at Mr. Hunt. Surely, he would tell the girls that this whole idea was nonsense! But instead of taking my side, he smiled, in obvious agreement with them.

"You must follow your destiny, Eric," he said.

After those words, we all sat quietly for a few moments. While the three of them were resting in serious contemplation, I suddenly stood up, acting as if I were about to leave them.

As I did that, Kathy asked, "Where are you going, Eric?"

"Oh, I thought I'd go down to the lagoon for awhile and practice walking on the water. Tell you what, folks," I said. "If I make it across, then I'll agree with you. But then the two of you girls will really have a job on your hands. You'll have to find ten other people who would like to join us as we walk up and down the shores of Lake Michigan."

Pam then said, "When you think of it like that, it does sound a bit 'far out,' doesn't it?"

Apparently, Kathy wasn't enjoying my humor, as she said, "Come on, Eric! Be serious!"

"Oh, I am being very serious, Kathy!" I replied. "Do you think I want to spend the next several years being laughed at and ridiculed by all my friends and other people? And then in the end, find myself nailed to some tree on a gloomy Friday afternoon in April?

"After all, I have an exciting life ahead of me."

Looking at the three of them, but nodding my head toward Kathy, I continued: "This beautiful young lady is soon going to be my wife. . . . And when I finish college next year, I'll either have an important position in my dad's company, or else I'll be able to put my marketing degree to good use by working for one of his suppliers."

Pam then spoke up: "Oh, that sounds real noble, Eric! Here you have an opportunity to really make a contribution to uplifting the consciousness of mankind. But, instead, you want to become just another faceless automaton who is lost in the sea of industrial and commercial mediocrity. Then some day when you make *your* 'transition', they'll remember you as the guy who at one time sold three-hundred-seventy-four widgets in a single year."

Hearing Pam describe it in that way, I realized that if any portion of what I had heard that day was true, it would be folly for me to try to live the rest of my life governed exclusively by human emotions and selfish personal desires. If I truly am a master, then I must follow the Master Christian's injunction to literally "become a servant."

We continued our discussion for another half hour. As we talked, Kathy appeared to be relishing the fact that she finally had found her heretofore anonymous guru. She was already making plans on how she could launch my new "career". And after having witnessed her zealous promoting of her tapes on "Primitive Christian Mysticism," I knew that my future was in good hands.

But even after all that had been said on that afternoon in the park, I still was fighting the inevitable direction in which this new revelation would have to lead me.

Understandably sensing my fears and doubts, Mr. Hunt asked if he could be of any further help at that time.

I replied, "Yes! Give me the information on how I can communicate with Shimahn!"

Once again, he reached into his pocket and pulled out a plain gray card. On this card was a brief description of an ashram located just outside the Tibetan capital of Lhasa. Mr. Hunt told us that the people in that ashram could direct us to Shimahn, who lived approximately sixty-five kilometers northeast of the city.

But then this spiritual seer repeated his belief that I didn't need another meeting with Shimahn.

"I'm sorry!" I said. "But if I'm going to accept this mission, even in a very small and limited way, I'll need to learn more about Truth . . . and Shimahn is the person who can teach me."

Mr. Hunt replied, "But all Truth is already established within yourself. You merely need to tap the hidden resources that exist at the very center of your own consciousness."

"But Shimahn has so much wisdom. I know that I can learn from him. . . ."

Kathy agreed with me: "I think Eric's right, Mr. Hunt. And I also would like to study with Shimahn."

Our wise old friend wouldn't give in, as he pressed his point: "You don't need to make that trip!"

"But Shimahn is my teacher!" I argued.

"That's not true!" he said.

"Then what is the truth?" I asked.

At that point, Jeremy Hunt made the two statements that virtually precluded the need for any further discussion—two statements that were to alter the course of my life forever.

He said, "Eric, you were Shimahn's spiritual teacher!"

Shocked by those words, I continued to resist: "How can that be? If I had acquired enough knowledge to have been his teacher, why wouldn't I show forth some of that in this present lifetime? And aside from that, Shimahn gained much of his wisdom from 'THE GOSPEL According to I AM'."

Gazing directly into my eyes, Mr. Hunt then said: "Eric . . . you were the author of 'THE GOSPEL'!"

Chapter Twelve

After Mr. Hunt had made those startling and unexpected statements, the four of us once again sat quietly on the grass. Both of the girls seemed to be extremely moved by his words. In fact, Kathy immediately closed her eyes and silently pondered what she had just heard.

I, too, experienced a number of different emotions, ranging from bewilderment, to denial, to disbelief. But Mr. Hunt had made those statements with such absolute conviction that none of us even considered questioning their authenticity.

After that brief interval of silence, the four of us rose from the grass and began walking out of the park. As we did that, I said: "Mr. Hunt, I think I understand what you've been telling us today—I'm not sure that I fully agree with all of your conclusions—but I do understand. . . . And I'm not ashamed to admit that all of this really frightens me."

"That's only natural, Eric," he replied. "This all has come as a rather sudden revelation to you."

"But I still don't accept your suggestion that I should be the 'anointed one'," I said. "I'm no better than anyone else."

"Oh, you're absolutely correct in that statement, Eric. You certainly are no better than anyone else. In fact, the moment you start believing that you are better will be the very moment when you take several steps backward in your spiritual unfoldment."

He then said, "It's not a question of being better or worse. Every person is the individualized expression of the Divine Consciousness and, therefore, every person is the Christ of God. Yet, while every one of us has this Christ within us, the degree to which we *recognize* our Christhood is the degree of our illumination.

"Every soul who has ever walked this earth has had that same divinity lying dormant within him or her, but most people have little or no awareness of it. . . . And that is where your work comes in."

Since we had left our meeting place in the park, neither of the girls had uttered a word. The three of us listened intently as Mr. Hunt continued:

"Eric, in previous life-experiences, you have achieved very high levels of spiritual awareness. Yet you, like all the rest of us, entered this present lifetime as what appears to be a very normal human being. But that is merely an appearance.

"In truth, you are a very special soul, Eric. Your progress on the 'path' has been extremely rapid. You didn't need hundreds of lifetimes to prepare yourself for this present experience. But now that you are here, you must accept your sacred mission. As you acknowledge your real Christ-identity, you will begin to peel away the veils of your humanhood—those human characteristics that are covering up this great light of Truth that you really are."

Mr. Hunt stopped walking at that point. Authoritatively looking into my eyes one last time, he then said, "As often as possible, study your 'GOSPEL'. You already know the Truth that is written there, but seeing it in print will bring it back to your mind, where it can become the 'Living Word.' Then meditate upon these truths and let them be confirmed within you."

Concluding that statement, Mr. Hunt shook my hand. Then turning toward Pam and Kathy, he said: "Now it will be up to you young ladies to keep Eric on the path. Remember, he has much to share with us, and he only needs to seek within himself to find it."

After those words, he smiled at the three of us, nodded his head, and quietly walked away. We stood motionless, watching him until he reached the corner, where he turned left and disappeared from our view.

Pam broke the silence by saying, "I wonder if we'll ever see him again?"

"Possibly," I replied. "But, I suspect, only if we ever have a real need for him."

That evening, the two girls and I spent our final night together in rather subdued conversation. Each of us was privately reflecting upon the significance of what we had heard that day.

During our flight home, my parents became aware of the taciturn introspection that Kathy and I were sharing. We assured them that there was no problem between us, but that we were both a little exhausted from the trip and just wanted to rest.

After spending the next three days with me at my parents' house, Kathy returned alone to Cincinnati by bus. During those three days together, our relationship seemed to undergo several minor changes. Openly, we were just as affectionate toward one another. But every now and then, I sensed a holding back in Kathy, as I caught her staring at me with a look of awe in her eyes. I tried to stress the fact that I still was the same person with whom she had fallen in love, and I told her that we shouldn't let Mr. Hunt's revelations affect our relationship. And aside from that, I reasoned, wasn't she the one who had been searching for some unknown master for the previous three years? Nonetheless, it had become readily apparent that Kathy needed some time alone so that she could get a clearer perspective of these events.

The final forty days of that summer vacation provided me with a needed opportunity for study and meditation. During that period, Kathy and I communicated by telephone about twice each week, but we spoke very little about spiritual Truth, and she never again mentioned the incident with Mr. Hunt.

While that forty-day period began as a somewhat ambiguous wilderness experience for me, I was able to practice and apply many of the mystical principles that I had learned in the past. As I did this, numerous passages in my "GOSPEL" became illuminated for me, and I instantaneously perceived the deep esoteric meaning of the words. Yet, in spite of the fact that I was receiving fresh inspiration daily, there were several times when my emotional state reached levels so low that I was tempted to irrevocably shirk my ultimate spiritual destiny and once again function as the "natural man," seeking my future happiness in the physical realm of cause and effect. But in each instance, I was able to overcome the temptation by recognizing the intrinsically fragile and temporal nature of a purely human existence. By that time, life without God-contact had become inconceivable to me. And even though I had many fears and concerns about my prophesied future mission in life, I had been able to achieve enough moments of peace during this period to mentally prepare myself for my upcoming final year of college.

Our return to Purdue University that fall seemed like a rebirth of our relationship. We started having fun again as Kathy and I spent most of our free time together. It was almost as if we never had left the campus and all the events of the summer hadn't happened. But even though Kathy never brought up the subject, I often thought about Mr. Hunt's disclosures, and I tried to keep my mind open and receptive to any directions along those lines that I might receive.

Then, on an unseasonably warm evening in early October, after lying in bed for several hours, I found myself having difficulty in falling asleep. As was my usual practice at such times, I read a few passages from "THE GOSPEL According to 'I AM'" and then closed my eyes and began contemplating Truth. After a few minutes of this conscious mental activity, my mind became still, and I achieved a point of absolute silence. In that state of meditative receptivity, I heard the words:

"'Thou art My beloved son in whom I am well pleased.' The time is now at hand for the new dispensation of grace and truth to be revealed. Many are hungering and thirsting after righteousness, yet their prayers will never be answered because they are praying amiss. Truth is already established within each person. It only needs to be recognized. This is the mystical message for this age: 'I AM That I AM'. But always remember that there is not I *and* thee. I am the Life of thy being . . . I am in thee and thou art in Me, for we are One . . . and this realization of Oneness is the ultimate revelation that must be given to all mankind."

After those words, the voice stopped speaking, and I was overcome by a deep sense of tranquility and assurance. Savoring that mystical moment, I rested in the Word and my mind was quiescent, not thinking any thoughts. I remained in that peaceful state for an immeasurable amount of time. But just before falling asleep, I began analyzing the message that I had received in my meditation. I wondered if this truly was a directive from "On High." Was I being told to start sharing my knowledge of Truth with others? Was this my foreordained moment of destiny?

The next evening, Kathy and I were doing homework together in the lounge of her dormitory. I wanted to tell her about my deep meditation experience of the previous night, but since we recently had spoken very little about spiritual matters, I didn't know how to bring up the subject. As things turned out, however, it wasn't necessary for me to say anything; because, after about an hour of routinely doing our homework, Kathy unexpectedly laid down her pencil and ominously looked into my eyes as she said:

"Eric, it came to me last night that now is the time to begin."

"Begin what?" I asked.

"Your ministry," she replied.

Somewhat lightheartedly, I said, "I thought we had forgotten all about that stuff by this time."

"You know better than that, Eric. We can never turn back."

"But you don't just 'start a ministry'," I said. "I don't have any training . . . nobody knows me . . . and I certainly haven't noticed any great clamoring out there for a new Messiah."

Kathy then said, "But late last night, I was having difficulty in falling asleep, so I sat up and read a few pages in "THE GOSPEL". I then went into a deep meditation and, after reaching a point of absolute silence, received instructions from the 'still, small voice.' I was told that *now* is the time to begin."

While I had had a similar revelation, I wanted to hear the rest of Kathy's story . . . and I didn't want to make this too easy for her. So with a twinkle in my eye, I kiddingly asked:

"Don't I even get a chance to retire into the wilderness for forty days and forty nights?"

"Very funny, Eric! But I am quite serious," she replied. "You've already had your chance in the wilderness. That's why I left you alone for the last month and a half of summer."

Inwardly, I was agreeing with all of Kathy's conclusions. But I didn't want to sound too eager, since I really was quite fearful of where this discussion was leading us. I then said:

"Okay! Let's assume that you're right, and *now* is the time. Where do we go. . . ? Who do I minister to?"

"We don't go anywhere! Your work will begin right here on the campus," she said. "This afternoon, I reserved Elizabeth Fowler Hall for the evening of November 1st. You'll give your first lecture at that time."

Reacting impetuously to those unexpected words, I knocked my chair over, as I leaped to my feet and shouted: "What do you mean, 'you reserved the hall'?"

Two other couples and another group of three girls were also sitting in the lounge at that time. When I raised my voice and created such a disturbance, they all stopped whatever they were doing and began staring at us. Since Kathy knew most of them, she merely waved her hand, signalling that everything was all right.

Regaining my composure, I repeated in a much softer voice: "What do you mean, 'you reserved the hall'?"

"I mean just that, Eric! We have to begin somewhere, and I believe that there are many students on the campus who will be receptive to Truth."

"Oh, sure!" I argued. "Just like the masses who have been coming to your tape-recorded lectures!"

"But this is different, Eric. You're a real live master, not just a voice on a tape. And aside from that, I know this is right. I was forcing the issue with my tapes. That was merely a human desire to share. And while my motives may have been proper, it still was nothing more than human willpower. This is divinely authorized. I have been told to do this!"

"But. . . ." I started to speak, but the words never came.

"Oh, Eric, I know how you must feel. Don't you think all of this scares me too? But when Mr. Hunt told me many years ago that you and I 'share a common spiritual destiny,' he wasn't just talking about us getting married some day. He was referring to this work that we must do."

What could I say? Knowing Kathy as I did, I realized that I wouldn't be able to talk her out of this undertaking. And her revelation merely confirmed the instructions that I had received in my own meditation. Maybe this was our time to begin.

In that moment, I could only think back to the words of the learned Pharisee Gamaliel: "For if this counsel or this work be of men, it will come to nought: But if it be of God, Ye cannot overthrow it."

Quietly acquiescing to my prophesied destiny, I allowed Kathy to go ahead with her plans to announce the event. I was able to console myself by the probability that no one would attend. If Kathy hadn't been able to attract anyone to her tape sessions when she presented a highly developed mystic like Shimahn, how could she entice anyone to come to a lecture by an unknown college student?

On Friday evening, November 1st, Kathy went to the lecture site early because she wanted to be there to welcome the guests. I decided that I would stay in my room meditating until the last moment. Then I would arrive at the hall precisely at the seven-thirty starting time.

As I approached the backstage entrance to Elizabeth Fowler Hall, one of Kathy's closest friends intercepted me.

"What are you doing here, Laurie?" I asked.

"I came to hear you speak," she said. "Uh . . . by the way, Kathy wants you to wait here while she introduces you."

I never had an opportunity to hear Kathy's introduction, but when she finished, Laurie signalled me to follow her into the hall. As I walked through the doorway, I became aware of a soft undercurrent of voices. This sound was gradually muted by polite applause, but by the time I reached the podium, the crowd's reaction had crescendoed to a deafening roar.

Looking out at the audience, I couldn't believe my eyes. Every single seat in the hall was filled. Though most of those in attendance were students, as I looked around I even noticed a few faculty members. "What did Kathy do?" I wondered. "Did she tell them that Billy Graham, or the Pope, was speaking tonight?"

Glancing around the room once more, I suddenly realized that there didn't appear to be an empty seat . . . and yet, no one was standing. Apparently, we had attracted an audience of the exact seating capacity of the hall—not one person more, and not one person less.

I then looked down at the front row where Kathy was sitting. Seated right next to her and holding her hand was my cousin Pamela. I had no idea that Pam was even aware of this lecture.

I smiled at the two girls who were both beaming from ear to ear. I then took a deep breath, looked out at the sea of faces, and said:

"Good evening, friends. . . ! Tonight, we're going to speak about the nature of your true identity. . . .

"To begin with . . . each one of you was created in the image and likeness of God. . . ."

The End

The Beginning

Part Two

The Gospel
According to "I AM"

CONTENTS...

CREATION
(Spiritual Unfoldment)

"In the beginning was the Word, and the Word was with God, and the Word was God.
The same was in the beginning with God.
All things were made by Him; and without Him was not any thing made that was made."

JOHN

"In the beginning God created the heaven and the earth.
And the earth was without form, and void; and darkness was upon the face of the deep. And the Spirit of God moved upon the face of the waters."

GENESIS

God is infinite Consciousness, the One Universal Life, the only Intelligence, Substance and Being. This omnipresent Divine Consciousness has always existed and will continue to exist throughout eternity. Therefore, the phrase "In the beginning" is a contradiction in terms. In absolute reality, there was no beginning. That which *Is* was never created, because a creation would imply a time when the *Is* was not.

Was there ever a time when two times two did not equal four? Was there ever a time when two parts of hydrogen combined with one part of oxygen did not produce water?

Every aspect of universal Truth has always existed. Truth, or God, is eternal. However, to a person conditioned by the false processes of the human mind, the concept of God expressing Himself forever—of immortal Life living, without beginning or ending—is quite difficult to accept. If we are consciously aware of nothing but finite physicality, we assume that every tangible object appearing in our human experience was created at some particular point in time and space. But absolute reality—the spiritual realm, or "My kingdom"—has no relationship to physical forms existing in time or space.

The true substance of this realm of Spirit is intangible to the human mentality and cannot be perceived by our five physical senses. Absolute reality can be discerned only by a transcendental, fourth-dimensional state of consciousness.

"And God said, 'Let there be light,' and there was light."

GENESIS

"In Him was life, and the life was the light of men."

JOHN

"And God saw the light, that it was good."

GENESIS

The writer of the Gospel of John refers to the "Logos" or "Word": "The Word was with God, and the Word was God." This Word is the eternal Truth of Being. It is the divine Self-knowledge of infinite Consciousness knowing Itself.

This divine Self-knowledge is also referred to as "light": "And God said, 'Let there be light,' and there was light. And God saw the light, that it was good." Therefore, the activity of Divine Consciousness knowing Itself constitutes the spiritual universe; and this activity never began and will never end.

God is . . . from everlasting to everlasting.

"That which was from the beginning, which we have heard, which we have seen with our eyes, which we have looked upon, and our hands have handled of the Word of life;

For the life was manifested, and we have seen it, and bear witness, and shew unto you that eternal life, which was with the Father, and was manifested unto us;

This then is the message which we have heard of him, and declare unto you, that God is light, and in Him is no darkness at all."

1st Epistle of JOHN

"I am Alpha and Omega, the beginning and the ending, saith the Lord, which is, and which was, and which is to come, the Almighty.

Thou art worthy, O Lord, to receive glory and honour and power: for Thou has created all things, and for Thy pleasure they are and were created."

JOHN of Patmos
As Recorded in REVELATION

"Know therefore this day, and consider it in thine heart, that the Lord He is God in heaven above, and upon the earth beneath: there is none else.

Hear, O Israel: The Lord our God is one Lord."

MOSES
As Recorded in DEUTERONOMY

"I am the Lord, and there is none else, there is no God beside Me: I girded thee, though thou hast not known Me:

That they may know from the rising of the sun, and from the west, that there is none beside Me. I am the Lord, and there is none else.

I have made the earth, and created man upon it: I, even My hands, have stretched out the heavens, and all their host have I commanded.

I have raised him up in righteousness, and I will direct all his ways."

ISAIAH

"The heavens declare the glory of God; and the firmament showeth His handiwork."

PSALM 19

"The earth is the Lord's and the fulness thereof."

PSALM 24

"Have we not all one Father? Hath not one God created us?"

MALACHI

"O the depth of the riches both of the wisdom and knowledge of God! How unsearchable are His judgements, and His ways past finding out!

For of Him, and through Him, and to Him, are all things."

PAUL
To the ROMANS

"*Know ye that the Lord He is God: it is He that hath made us, and not we ourselves.*"

PSALM 100

"*For every house is builded by some man; but He that built all things is God.*"

HEBREWS

"'*Am I a God at hand,' saith the Lord, 'and not a God afar off? Do not I fill heaven and earth?' saith the Lord.*"

JEREMIAH

"*For the word of the Lord is right, and all His works are done in truth.*
... the earth is full of the goodness of the Lord.
By the word of the Lord were the heavens made; and all the host of them by the breath of His mouth.
For He spake, and it was done; He commanded, and it stood fast."

PSALM 33

"*I call heaven and earth to record this day against you, that I have set before you life and death, blessing and cursing: therefore choose life, that both thou and thy seed may live:*
That thou mayest love the Lord thy God ... for He is thy life, and the length of thy days."

MOSES
As Recorded in DEUTERONOMY

"For by [God] were all things created, that are in heaven, and that are in earth, visible and invisible, whether they be thrones, or dominions, or principalities, or powers: all things were created by Him, and for Him:
And He is before all things, and by Him all things consist."

PAUL
To the COLOSSIANS

God is the basic creative Principle of all that exists; but Principle is not separate from Its manifestation. There is not God *and* a creation; there is not Consciousness *and* an expression. God is the Substance of all form. This universal Divine Consciousness is unfolding Itself, revealing and disclosing Itself, *as* the spiritual universe.

God, the One infinite, all-inclusive Being, is individually expressing Itself *as* the spiritual identity of every person who ever has appeared, or who ever will appear, on earth.

"I AM That I AM" is the dictum of Spirit. . . .

"There is one body, and one Spirit...
One God and Father of all, who is above all, and through all, and in you all."

PAUL
To the EPHESIANS

"I know that, whatsoever God doeth, it shall be forever: nothing can be put to it, nor any thing taken from it."

ECCLESIASTES

IDENTITY
(The Son of God & The Son of Man)

THE SON OF GOD

"And God said, 'Let Us make man in Our image, after Our likeness: and let them have dominion over the fish of the sea, and over the fowl of the air, and over the cattle, and over every creeping thing that creepeth upon the earth.'

So God created man in His own image, in the image of God created He him; male and female created He them.

And God blessed them, and God said unto them, 'Be fruitful, and multiply, and replenish the earth and subdue it.'"

GENESIS

"And Moses said unto God, 'Behold, when I come unto the children of Israel, and shall say unto them, The God of your fathers hath sent me unto you; and they shall say to me, What is His name? What shall I say unto them?'

And God said unto Moses, 'I AM That I AM': and He said, 'Thus shalt thou say unto the children of Israel, I AM hath sent me unto you.'"

EXODUS

"Verily, verily, I say unto you, Before Abraham was, I am."

CHRIST JESUS
As Recorded by JOHN

"But now, thus saith the Lord that created thee . . . 'Fear not: for I have redeemed thee, I have called thee by thy name; thou art Mine.

'I am with thee: I will bring thy seed from the east, and gather thee from the west.

'I will say to the north . . . and to the south . . . bring My sons from far, and My daughters from the ends of the earth.

'Even every one that is called by My name: for I have created him for My glory.'

'Ye are My witnesses,' saith the Lord, 'that I am God.'"

ISAIAH

"Philip saith unto him, 'Lord, shew us the Father, and it sufficeth us.'

Jesus saith unto him, 'Have I been so long time with you, and yet hast thou not known me, Philip? He that hath seen me hath seen the Father; and how sayest thou then, Shew us the Father?

'Believest thou not that I am in the Father, and the Father in me? The words that I speak unto you I speak not of myself: but the Father that dwelleth in me, He doeth the works.

'*Believe me that I am in the Father, and the Father in me.*
'*I and my Father are one.*'

These words spake Jesus . . . '*And now, O Father, glorify Thou me with Thine own Self, with the glory which I had with Thee before the world was.*

'*I have manifested Thy name unto the men which Thou gavest me out of the world: Thine they were, and Thou gavest them me.*

'*They are not of the world, even as I am not of the world.*

'*Neither pray I for these alone, but for them also which shall believe on me through their word;*

'*That they all may be one; as Thou, Father, art in me, and I in Thee, that they also may be one in us:*

'*And the glory which Thou gavest me I have given them; that they may be one, even as we are one:*

'*I in them, and Thou in me, that they may be made perfect in one.*'"

CHRIST JESUS
As Recorded by JOHN

"*For the law was given by Moses, but grace and truth came by Jesus Christ.*"

JOHN

The Master's new dispensation of grace and truth is a total recognition of absolute oneness.

The ancient Hebrews declared: "Hear, O Israel: The Lord our God is one Lord." They accepted one God, one Creator. But Jesus expanded this concept of oneness to include all mankind. He was consciously aware of his own unity with the Father: "I and my Father are One." But he also realized that all men are one by virtue of their divine sonship: "that they may be one, even as we are one: I in them, and Thou in me, that they may be made perfect in one."

"Thou art My beloved Son, in whom I am well pleased."

MARK

"Behold what manner of love the Father hath bestowed upon us, that we should be called the sons of God: therefore the world knoweth us not, because it knew Him not.

Beloved, now are we the sons of God, and it doth not yet appear what we shall be: but we know that when He shall appear, we shall be like Him; for we shall see Him as He is."

1st Epistle of JOHN

"Son, thou art ever with Me, and all that I have is thine."

LUKE

"*The Spirit Itself beareth witness with our spirit, that we are the children of God:*

And if children, then heirs; heirs of God, and joint-heirs with Christ."

PAUL
To the ROMANS

"*Call no man your father upon the earth: for One is your Father, which is in heaven.*"

CHRIST JESUS
As Recorded by MATTHEW

God the Father becomes manifest as God the Son. Divine Consciousness is unfolding and revealing Itself as individual consciousness. Therefore, your true identity is the "Son of God."

As the wave is one with the ocean, and as the flame is one with the fire, so is the Son one with the Father. As joint-heir with Christ, your real identity includes every quality and attribute of the Godhead. Divine Consciousness is the essence and substance of your being. Your body is actually the spiritual embodiment of every aspect of God.

"*But God giveth it a body as it hath pleased Him, and to every seed His own body.*

Know ye not that your body is the temple of the Holy Ghost which is in you?

Know ye not that ye are the temple of God, and that the Spirit of God dwelleth in you?"

PAUL
To the CORINTHIANS

"[Jesus] asked his disciples, saying, 'Whom do men say that I the Son of Man am?'
And they said, 'Some say that thou art John the Baptist, some, Elias; and others, Jeremias, or one of the prophets.'
He saith unto them, 'But whom say ye that I am?'
And Simon Peter answered and said, 'Thou art the Christ, the Son of the Living God.'"

MATTHEW

"And all things are of God, who hath reconciled us to Himself by Jesus Christ. . .
. . .God was in Christ, reconciling the world unto Himself. . .
Therefore if any man be in Christ, he is a new creature: old things are passed away; behold, all things are become new."

PAUL
To the CORINTHIANS

Christ is the only begotten Son of God. But the Christ was not a personal characteristic belonging exclusively to Jesus. The Christ is the true divine identity of every child of God; and this identity, which really is the individualization of God's Own Being, has existed and will continue to exist throughout eternity.

Our recognition and acceptance of these facts will bring the Christ and its redemptive power into our personal experience. But before we can share in the glory of Christhood, we must "die" to our false sense of life and be reborn of the Spirit. We must surrender all belief in a selfhood apart from God and be purged of all human opinions, desires, ambitions and fears. Then, from our newly developed state of spiritual awareness, will we recognize our own divine sonship and be able to say with the Master: "I and my Father are One."

"For we are His workmanship, created in Christ Jesus."

> *PAUL*
> *To the EPHESIANS*

"Lie not one to another, seeing that ye have put off the old man with his deeds;

And have put on the new man, which is renewed in knowledge after the image of Him that created him."

> *PAUL*
> *To the COLOSSIANS*

"So we, being many, are one body in Christ, and every one members one of another.

There is therefore now no condemnation to them which are in Christ Jesus, who walk not after the flesh, but after the Spirit.

For the law of the Spirit of life in Christ Jesus hath made me free from the law of sin and death.

But ye are not in the flesh, but in the Spirit, if so be that the Spirit of God dwell in you. . .

For as many as are led by the Spirit of God, they are the sons of God."

PAUL
To the ROMANS

"The Lord thy God in the midst of thee is mighty."

ZEPHANIAH

"God that made the world and all things therein, seeing that He is Lord of heaven and earth, dwelleth not in temples made with hands;

Neither is worshipped with men's hands, as though He needed any thing, seeing He giveth to all life, and breath, and all things;

For in Him we live, and move, and have our being; as certain also of your own poets have said, For we are also His offspring."

PAUL
To the Athenians
(on Mars Hill) ACTS

"Ye are of God, little children, and have overcome them: because greater is He that is in you, than he that is in the world.

If we love one another, God dwelleth in us, and His love is perfected in us.

Hereby know we that we dwell in Him, and He in us, because He has given us of His Spirit."

1st Epistle of JOHN

In addition to having "given us of His Spirit," God has also given us His name. And that name, which was first revealed to Moses, is "I AM".

Since God is infinite, this One all-inclusive Consciousness is expressing Itself individually as the *I* of our being. God, the great "I AM", is appearing as *I*, the Christ, and this is the true spiritual *I*-dentity of each one of us.

Jesus had a clear and absolute recognition of his Christhood. Therefore, whenever he referred to his divine *I*-dentity, he used the word "*I*" in its highest connotation:

"Then spake Jesus again unto them, saying, 'I am the light of the world. . .

'I have meat to eat that ye know not of.

'Whosoever drinketh of this water shall thirst again:

'But whosoever drinketh of the water that I shall give him shall never thirst; but the water that I shall give him shall be in him a well of water springing up into everlasting life.

'I am the bread of life: he that cometh to me shall never hunger, and he that believeth on me shall never thirst."

CHRIST JESUS
As Recorded by JOHN

What comfort and confidence these words hold for mankind! Yet, contrary to the Master's assurances, many of his followers have hungered and thirsted. There are several specific reasons for this seeming contradiction.

The scriptural word which has been translated as "believe" had a much broader meaning when it was spoken by Jesus in his original Aramaic language. Unlike our present-day definition, which implies faith or blind belief, the Master's use of that word denoted more than mere faith: an understanding or discernment of his teaching. Therefore, in order for us to partake in the fruitage of his sacred ministry, we must relinquish our personal worship of Jesus the man and, rather, follow his directive to seek the kingdom of God that exists within our own consciousness.

This Nazarene carpenter certainly realized that, as the human Jesus, he didn't have the power to heal the sick, raise the dead, or feed the multitudes: "I can of mine own self do nothing."

But when he was functioning as the Christ, the only begotten Son of God, the Master knew that he could allude to his divine *I*-dentity and, therein, adopt the name of God as his own. Hence his declarations: "*I* am the light of the world," "*I* am the bread of life," etc.

In these statements, Jesus is telling us that the Christ—the divine *I* within him—is the "light of the world" and the "bread of life." But an in-depth study of the words and works of the Master will reveal that he never claimed this divine *I*-ness as his own personal and exclusive possession.

Jesus often taught that all those who believe (understand) his message will participate in the glorious splendor of divine sonship: "that they may be one, even as we are one. . . ."

The esoteric meaning of Christ's teaching reveals that *I* is the name of the spiritual Son of God, and this *I* resides within each of us. Accordingly, he instructs us to make contact with this Reality of our own being and allow It to teach us, feed us and sustain us.

"Be of good cheer: It is I; be not afraid."

CHRIST JESUS
As Recorded by MARK

"Jesus said unto them, 'Verily, verily, I say unto you, Before Abraham was, I am.

'And I, if I be lifted up from the earth, will draw all men unto me.

'I am the resurrection and the life:

'I am come that they might have life, and that they might have it more abundantly.'"

CHRIST JESUS
As Recorded by JOHN

"I am the true vine, and my Father is the husbandman.

Every branch in me that beareth not fruit He taketh away: and every branch that beareth fruit, He purgeth it, that it may bring forth more fruit.

Abide in me, and I in you. As the branch cannot bear fruit of itself, except it abide in the vine; no more can ye, except ye abide in me.

I am the vine, ye are the branches: He that abideth in me, and I in him, the same bringeth forth much fruit: for without me ye can do nothing.

If a man abide not in me, he is cast forth as a branch, and is withered; and men gather them, and cast them into the fire, and they are burned.

If ye abide in me, and my words abide in you, ye shall ask what ye will, and it shall be done unto you.

Herein is my Father glorified, that ye bear much fruit."

CHRIST JESUS
As Recorded by JOHN

I, the Christ within you, is the vine—the universal "tree of life." When you recognize and accept your divine Sonship as this I, you are in unity with all life. However, living as the "man of earth" and believing that you have a selfhood apart from God, you are as a branch that is cut off from this tree of life; a branch that is withering and dying.

"Awake thou that sleepest." You have the capacity to rise above all the limitations of "this world." Accept your God-given dominion over all things. This is your divine birthright as the image and likeness of Infinite Spirit. "Thou art the Christ, the Son of the living God." Realize that "I am in the Father, and the Father [is] in me." Acknowledge and accept your divine Sonship as I, the Christ. Meditate upon this wondrous Truth and let the I in the midst of you reveal Itself.

"I live; yet not I, but Christ liveth in me."

PAUL
To the GALATIANS

"Come unto me, all ye that labour and are heavy laden, and I will give you rest."

CHRIST JESUS
As Recorded by MATTHEW

"I am the way, the truth, and the life: no man cometh unto the Father, but by me."

CHRIST JESUS
As Recorded by JOHN

"Be still, and know that I am God."

Psalm 46

"Lo, I am with you alway, even unto the end of the world."

CHRIST JESUS
As Recorded by MATTHEW

THE SON OF MAN

"The son of man cometh at an hour when ye think not."

CHRIST JESUS
As Recorded by LUKE

As the image and likeness of God, man is the individualized expression of Infinite Spirit. This real man, or Christ identity, is perfect, "even as [the] Father in heaven is perfect." But the human mind has accepted a false concept of this spiritual identity. Consequently, mankind is seeing God's perfect creation through distorted vision. As the Apostle Paul described it: we are seeing [our world] "through a glass darkly."

To justify and explain this false sense of existence, the second chapter of Genesis presents an allegorical account of creation:

"And the Lord God formed man of the dust of the ground, and breathed into his nostrils the breath of life; and man became a living soul."

GENESIS

"Cease ye from man, whose breath is in his nostrils: for wherein is he to be accounted of?"

ISAIAH

"And the Lord God caused a deep sleep to fall upon Adam, and he slept: and He took one of his ribs, and closed up the flesh instead thereof;

And [out of] the rib, which the Lord God had taken from man, made He a woman, and brought her unto the man.

And Adam said, 'This is now bone of my bones, and flesh of my flesh: she shall be called Woman, because she was taken out f Man."

GENESIS

According to this allegory, mankind [Adam] was created rom the dust of the ground. Unlike the image and likeness of iod—that perfect man described in the first chapter of ienesis—Adam represents an illusory concept of life that is ›ased upon material sense testimony. This concept presumes a reation separate and apart from the Creator. But Infinite 'onsciousness and Its manifestation are One. There is not God nd a creation. There is not God *and* man.

God, the Father, expresses and reveals Himself ›dividually *as* God, the Son.

For this reason, any claim of a selfhood disconnected om its Source is an illusion. The "man of earth"—the fleshly ›ortal who appears to this world of material sense—has no xistence in absolute reality:

"All flesh is grass."

ISAIAH

"Watch ye and pray, lest ye enter into temptation. The spirit truly is ready, but the flesh is weak."

CHRIST JESUS
As Recorded by MARK

"It is the Spirit that quickeneth; the flesh profiteth nothing."

CHRIST JESUS
As Recorded by JOHN

"For ye see your calling, brethren, how that not many wise men after the flesh, not many mighty, not many noble, are called:

But God hath chosen the foolish things of the world to confound the wise; and God hath chosen the weak things of the world to confound the things which are mighty;

That no flesh should glory in His presence.

Wherefore, henceforth know we no man after the flesh.

For as in Adam all die, even so in Christ shall all be made alive."

PAUL
To the CORINTHIANS

The Master, Christ Jesus, realized that he often exhibited a dual nature. His true identity was the Christ—that part of him that was divine. But, in order to fulfill his spiritual destiny as the Wayshower, he also appeared to mankind as the human Jesus—the carpenter's son who later became a Hebrew rabbi. Recognizing the limitations of his mortal sense of life, the Master frequently showed his disdain for his human nature:

"But Jesus answered them, 'My Father worketh hitherto, and I work.

'Verily, verily, I say unto you, the Son can do nothing of himself, but what he seeth the Father do: for what things soever He doeth, these also doeth the Son likewise.

'I can of mine own self do nothing:
'If I bear witness of myself, my witness is not true."

CHRIST JESUS
As Recorded by JOHN

"Why callest thou me good? There is none good but One, that is, God."

CHRIST JESUS
As Recorded by MATTHEW

"There is a natural body, and there is a spiritual body.

And so it is written, the first man Adam was made a living soul; the last Adam was made a quickening spirit.

Howbeit that was not first which is spiritual, but that which is natural; and afterward that which is spiritual.

The first man is of the earth, earthy: the second man is the Lord from heaven.

As is the earthy, such are they also that are earthy: and as is the heavenly, such are they also that are heavenly.

And as we have borne the image of the earthy, we shall also bear the image of the heavenly.

Now this I say, brethren, 'that flesh and blood cannot inherit the Kingdom of God.'"

PAUL
To the CORINTHIANS

Throughout most of recorded history, mankind has undertaken a futile mission to understand and overcome its own mortality. But through all these centuries, only a select few highly enlightened souls have been able to break through the mist of material sense.

Moses, standing before the burning bush on Mt. Horeb, learned that the real nature of his existence was "I AM", which also is the name and nature of God. Gautama the Buddha, after years of searching for the cause of sickness, old age and death, discovered that these things are "maya" or illusion. Jesus realized that his true identity was the Christ (which is another name for the "I AM" of Moses) and that his human nature was virtually insignificant. The Master knew that he could surrender his human sense of life at any time, and the *I* within his consciousness could then resurrect it again:

"I lay down my life, that I might take it again.
No man taketh it from me, but I lay it down myself.
I have power to lay it down, and I have power to take it again.
Destroy this temple, and in three days I will raise it up."

CHRIST JESUS
As Recorded by JOHN

"For we know that if our earthly house of this tabernacle were dissolved, we have a building of God, an house not made with hands, eternal in the heavens.

For in this we groan, earnestly desiring to be clothed upon with our house which is from heaven:

If so be that being clothed we shall not be found naked.

For we that are in this tabernacle do groan, being burdened: not that we would be unclothed, but clothed upon, that mortality might be swallowed up of life.

Therefore we are always confident, knowing that, whilst we are at home in the body, we are absent from the Lord."

PAUL
To the CORINTHIANS

Paul also made a distinction between the Son of God—that spiritual being described in the first chapter of Genesis—and the illusory concept of man which is perceived by the five physical senses. He realized that the "man of earth" exists in a supposititious realm, separate and apart from the Consciousness that is God. This discerning apostle referred to the person functioning under this human sense of life as "the natural man."

"But as it is written, Eye hath not seen, nor ear heard, neither have entered into the heart of man, the things which God hath prepared for them that love Him.

But God hath revealed them unto us by His Spirit: for the Spirit searcheth all things, yea, the deep things of God.

For what man knoweth the things of a man, save the spirit of man which is in him? Even so the things of God knoweth no man, but the Spirit of God.

Now we have received, not the spirit of the world, but the Spirit which is of God; that we might know the things that are freely given to us of God.

But the natural man receiveth not the things of the Spirit of God: for they are foolishness unto him: neither can he know them, because they are spiritually discerned."

PAUL
To the CORINTHIANS

"This I say then, Walk in the Spirit, and ye shall not fulfil the lust of the flesh.

For the flesh lusteth against the Spirit, and the Spirit against the flesh: and these are contrary the one to the other: so that ye cannot do the things that ye would.

But if ye be led of the Spirit, ye are not under the law.

But the fruit of the Spirit is love, joy, peace, longsuffering, gentleness, goodness, faith,

Meekness, temperance: against such there is no law.

If we live in the Spirit, let us also walk in the Spirit.

Bear ye one another's burdens, and so fulfil the law of Christ.

For if a man think himself to be something, when he is nothing, he deceiveth himself.

Be not deceived: God is not mocked: for whatsoever a man soweth, that shall he also reap.

For he that soweth to his flesh shall of the flesh reap corruption; but he that soweth to the Spirit shall of the Spirit reap life everlasting."

PAUL
To the GALATIANS

"This I say therefore, and testify in the Lord, that ye henceforth walk not as other Gentiles walk, in the vanity of their mind,

Having the understanding darkened, being alienated from the life of God through the ignorance that is in them, because of the blindness of their heart:

But ye have not so learned Christ;

If so be that ye have heard him, and have been taught by him, as the truth is in Jesus:

That ye put off concerning the former conversation the old man, which is corrupt according to the deceitful lusts;

And be renewed in the spirit of your mind;

And that ye put on the new man, which after God is created in righteousness and true holiness.

PAUL
To the EPHESIANS

"For they that are after the flesh do mind the things of the flesh; but they that are after the Spirit the things of the Spirit.

For to be carnally minded is death; but to be spiritually minded is life and peace.

Because the carnal mind is enmity against God; for it is not subject to the law of God, neither indeed can be.

So then they that are in the flesh cannot please God.

But if the Spirit of Him that raised up Christ from the dead shall also quicken your mortal bodies by His Spirit that dwelleth in you.

Therefore, brethren, we are debtors, not to the flesh, to live after the flesh.

For if ye live after the flesh, ye shall die: but if ye through the Spirit do mortify the deeds of the body, ye shall live.

For as many as are led by the Spirit of God, they are the sons of God.

For I reckon that the sufferings of this present time are not worthy to be compared with the glory which shall be revealed in us.

For the earnest expectation of the creature waiteth for the manifestation of the sons of God.

For the creature was made subject to vanity, not willingly, but by reason of him who hath subjected the same in hope,

Because the creature itself also shall be delivered from the bondage of corruption into the glorious liberty of the children of God."

PAUL
To the ROMANS

REALITY AND ILLUSION
("My Kingdom" and "This World")

"My kingdom is not of this world."

CHRIST JESUS
As Recorded by JOHN

"The kingdom of God cometh not with observation:
Neither shall they say, Lo here! or, lo there! for, behold, the
kingdom of God is within you."

CHRIST JESUS
As Recorded by LUKE

Jesus clearly understood that there is a spiritual realm of reality which he referred to as "My kingdom" or "the kingdom of God." But he also realized that, to the human mentality, there appears to be a hypothetical physical realm which he referred to as "this world."

The Master told us that the kingdom of God cannot be found in externals—in the conceptual world of cause and effect. Instead, he promised that we will discover this divine kingdom if we turn to the spiritual center of our own being.

The kingdom of God exists within our individual consciousness; in fact, the kingdom of God actually is the very fiber and fabric of our consciousness. But by falsely usurping the name of God, the universal human mind claims that this is not the case.

However, we are capable of rising above this false claim because, in absolute reality, the human mind does not even exist. This pseudo-mind is not the seat of intelligence; it has no creative power. This false-sense-of-mind is merely a counterfeit of the Divine Consciousness which is individually expressing Itself as our true identity. And, yet, the human mind surreptitiously pretends to be the arena in which the conflicting forces of "this world" are doing battle. But we do not have to be a party to this battleground of conflicting forces.

"For the prince of this world cometh, and hath nothing in me.

In the world ye shall have tribulation: but be of good cheer; I have overcome the world.

And now I am no more in the world, but these are in the world, and I come to Thee. Holy Father, keep through Thine Own name those whom Thou hast given me, that they may be one, as we are.

While I was with them in the world, I kept them in Thy name...

I have given them Thy word; and the world hath hated them, because they are not of the world, even as I am not of the world."

CHRIST JESUS
As Recorded by JOHN

"And be not conformed to this world: but be ye transformed by the renewing of your mind, that ye may prove what is that good, and acceptable, and perfect, will of God."

PAUL
To the ROMANS

"Let no man deceive himself. If any man among you seemeth to be wise in this world, let him become a fool, that he may be wise.

For the wisdom of this world is foolishness with God...

While we look not at the things which are seen, but at the things which are not seen: for the things which are seen are temporal; but the things which are not seen are eternal."

PAUL
To the CORINTHIANS

"My kingdom"—that realm of spiritual reality described by Jesus—exists in a fourth dimension and cannot be perceived by our five physical senses. Hence, Paul's admonition for us to "be not conformed to this world: but [to] be . . . transformed by the renewing of [our] mind." This renewal process is an activity of consciousness in which we "die daily" to the false sense of life under which we have been functioning. It is a surrendering of all faith in matter and material laws, and an ultimate awakening to our true identity as the perfect expression of God's Being.

As we begin to function from this new frame-of-reference, we discover that our interests and desires are changing. Many of the things that motivated us in the past have little effect on us today. And, as we continue to grow in spiritual awareness, the various "princes of this world" can come to us, but they receive little or no response from us.

"Lay not up for yourselves treasures upon earth, where moth and rust doth corrupt, and where thieves break through and steal:

But lay up for yourselves treasures in heaven, where neither moth nor rust doth corrupt, and where thieves do not break through nor steal:

For where your treasure is, there will your heart be also."

CHRIST JESUS
As Recorded by MATTHEW

"Therefore I say unto you, Take no thought for your life, what ye shall eat; neither for the body, what ye shall put on.

The life is more than meat, and the body is more than raiment.

Consider the ravens: for they neither sow nor reap; which neither have storehouse nor barn; and God feedeth them: how much more are ye better than the fowls?

And which of you with taking thought can add to his stature one cubit?

If ye then be not able to do that thing which is least, why take ye thought for the rest?

Consider the lilies how they grow: they toil not, they spin not; and yet I say unto you, that Solomon in all his glory was not arrayed like one of these.

If then God so clothe the grass, which is today in the field, and tomorrow is cast into the oven; how much more will He clothe you, O ye of little faith?

And seek not ye what ye shall eat, or what ye shall drink, neither be ye of doubtful mind.

For all these things do the nations of the world seek after: and your Father knoweth that ye have need of these things.

But rather seek ye the kingdom of God; and all these things shall be added unto you."

CHRIST JESUS
As Recorded by LUKE

The "man of earth" is concerned primarily with circumstances and conditions that affect his personal body or immediate environment. This mortal-sense-of-man is functioning exclusively at a physical level of awareness and, consequently, is always striving to improve its physical surroundings.

But this world of material sense is an illusion!

So when we place our faith in, or attempt to change, the outer appearances of our life, we are dealing with effects and, by reason of that, are merely trying to patch up illusions.

In his Sermon on the Mount, Christ Jesus told us not to be concerned with the things of this world. He instructed us to "seek . . . the kingdom of God." Then he followed that directive with the promise that, when we find this kingdom within our own consciousness, "all these things will be added unto [us]."

In general, mankind never has been willing to accept this most fundamental teaching of the Master. Mortal man has become a reactionary. He reacts to events of "this world." He has lost sight of his divine birthright as the reflected likeness of God and has forsaken the inner kingdom to dwell exclusively in the outer realm of human appearances.

"Judge not according to the appearance, but judge righteous judgement."

CHRIST JESUS
As Recorded by JOHN

"And the Lord God said, 'It is not good that the man should be alone; I will make him an help meet for him.'

And out of the ground the Lord God formed every beast of the field, and every fowl of the air; and brought them unto Adam to see what he would call them: and whatsoever Adam called every living creature, that was the name thereof.

And Adam gave names to all the cattle, and to the fowl of the air, and to every beast of the field; but for Adam there was not found an help meet for him.

And the Lord God caused a deep sleep to fall upon Adam, and he slept. . . ."

GENESIS

According to the allegory in the second chapter of Genesis, Adam (the false concept of man) was allowed to give names to every living creature. Following this precedent, the "man of earth" today is still labeling all the objects, circumstances and conditions of his universe; but not perceiving the unreality of this physical plane of life, mankind has unwittingly reverted back to Adam's practice of "judging by appearances."

The Genesis narrative then tells us that "the Lord God caused a deep sleep to fall upon Adam." In this fable, we are given no indication that Adam has ever been awakened from this "deep sleep." That is why humanhood, or the material sense of life, has often been referred to as the "Adam dream."

"Awake thou that sleepest, and arise from the dead, and Christ shall give thee light."

PAUL
To the EPHESIANS

"As for me, I will behold Thy face in righteousness: I shall be satisfied, when I awake, with Thy likeness."

PSALM 17

"And that, knowing the time, that now it is high time to awake out of sleep...
The night is far spent, the day is at hand: let us therefore cast off the works of darkness, and let us put on the armour of light."

PAUL
To the ROMANS

"How long wilt thou sleep, O sluggard? When wilt thou arise out of thy sleep?"

PROVERBS

"Ye are all the children of light, and the children of the day: we are not of the night, nor of darkness.
Therefore let us not sleep, as do others...
For they that sleep, sleep in the night...
But let us, who are of the day, be sober, putting on the breastplate of faith and love."

PAUL
To the THESSALONIANS

As human beings, we are functioning under the influence of the "Adam dream." But, in our immaculate true identity, we are not human beings. After we awaken to this fact, our spiritual journey begins, and our daily life becomes a series of progressive unfoldments. From that point forward, we experience total fulfillment as states and stages of unfolding awareness. As we "die daily" to our false sense of existence, we eventually come to realize that our greatest desire is to know God aright, and this will be our key to eternal life:

"And this is life eternal, that they might know Thee the only true God, and Jesus Christ, whom Thou hast sent."

CHRIST JESUS
As Recorded by JOHN

"He that findeth his life shall lose it: and he that loseth his life for my sake shall find it."

CHRIST JESUS
As Recorded by MATTHEW

"He that loveth his life shall lose it; and he that hateth his life in this world shall keep it unto life eternal."

CHRIST JESUS
As Recorded by JOHN

GOOD AND EVIL
(The Pairs of Opposites)

"And God saw every thing that He had made, and, behold, it was very good."

GENESIS

"Thou art of purer eyes than to behold evil, and canst not look on iniquity."

HABAKKUK

"And the Lord God planted a garden eastward in Eden; and there He put the man whom He had formed.

And out of the ground made the Lord God to grow every tree that is pleasant to the sight, and good for food; the tree of life also in the midst of the garden, and the tree of knowledge of good and evil.

And the Lord God took the man, and put him into the garden of Eden to dress it and to keep it.

And the Lord God commanded the man, saying, 'Of every tree of the garden thou mayest freely eat:

'But of the tree of the knowledge of good and evil, thou shalt not eat of it: for in the day that thou eatest thereof thou shalt surely die."'

GENESIS

The spiritual record of creation in the first chapter of Genesis tells us that "God saw every thing that He had made, and, behold, it was very good."

Contrary to this account, the allegory in Genesis 2 refutes this depiction of a perfect creation by implying that the one all-inclusive Consciousness is capable of showing Itself forth in some limited or defective way.

The truth is that God is aware of nothing but Its Own infinite Self-containment. Divine Consciousness is eternally revealing and disclosing the perfection of Its Own Being, and this activity of Consciousness unfolding is what constitutes the spiritual universe. Therefore, this real universe of Spirit must exhibit all the characteristics of the Godhead. As the Bible describes it: everything created by God was "very good."

How, then, can we reconcile this perfect spiritual creation with all the evil circumstances that come into our lives?

If God is omnipresent and is wholly good, then, in our real life-experience, there is no possibility for evil to appear, except as an illusion—as an implied opposite to the ever-present allness of good. But because of mankind's long-standing preoccupation with these pairs of opposites, the scriptural writers of antiquity have given us many conflicting statements on the subject of good and evil.

For this reason, it is imperative for us to develop a spiritually enlightened consciousness if we wish to discern the hidden Truth that has been chronicled in the Bible and other scriptural writings.

"Every good gift and every perfect gift is from above, and cometh down from the Father of lights, with whom is no variableness, neither shadow of turning."

JAMES

"Now the serpent was more subtil than any beast of the field which the Lord God had made. And he said unto the woman, 'Yea, hath God said, "Ye shall not eat of every tree of the garden?"'

And the woman said unto the serpent, 'We may eat of the fruit of the trees of the garden:

'But of the fruit of the tree which is in the midst of the garden, God hath said, "Ye shall not eat of it, neither shall ye touch it, lest ye die."'

And the serpent said unto the woman, 'Ye shall not surely die:

'For God doth know that in the day ye eat thereof, then your eyes shall be opened, and ye shall be as gods, knowing good and evil.'

And when the woman saw that the tree was good for food, and that it was pleasant to the eyes, and a tree to be desired to make one wise, she took of the fruit thereof, and did eat, and gave also unto her husband with her; and he did eat.

And the eyes of them both were opened, and they knew that they were naked; and they sewed fig leaves together, and made themselves aprons.

And they heard the voice of the Lord God walking in the garden in the cool of the day: and Adam and his wife hid themselves from the presence of the Lord God amongst the trees of the garden.

And the Lord God called unto Adam, and said unto him, 'Where art thou?'

And he said, 'I heard Thy voice in the garden, and I was afraid, because I was naked; and I hid myself.'

And He said, 'Who told thee that thou wast naked? Hast thou eaten of the tree, whereof I commanded thee that thou shouldest not eat?'

And the man said, 'The woman whom Thou gavest to be with me, she gave me of the tree, and I did eat.'

And the Lord God said unto the woman, 'What is this that thou hast done?' And the woman said, 'The serpent beguiled me, and I did eat.'"

GENESIS

Again, the allegorical Garden of Eden story presents a false concept of God, in which the Infinite Invisible is portrayed as a man-like being with human emotions, opinions and characteristics. This "Lord God" of the Genesis metaphor is not the Divine Principle of the universe, but is merely an ancient author's concept of a God who rewards and punishes, who judges and condemns, and who is aware of good and evil.

Certainly, this is not the same God that James describes as: "the Father of lights, with whom is no variableness, neither shadow of turning." Neither is this the Supreme Being that Habakkuk said is "of purer eyes than to behold evil"; nor is it the Deity described in the First Epistle of John: "God is Love."

The "Lord God" of this mythological account of creation also is not the one universal Consciousness, who "saw every thing that He had made, and, behold, it was very good." In fact, this "Lord God" really is not God at all but, rather, is merely another name for Karmic law—the law of "as ye sow, so shall ye reap."

"For whatsoever a man soweth, that shall he also reap.

For he that soweth to his flesh shall of the flesh reap corruption; but he that soweth to the Spirit shall of the Spirit reap life everlasting."

PAUL
To the GALATIANS

"Even as I have seen, they that plow iniquity, and sow wickedness, reap the same."

ELIPHAZ The Temanite
As Recorded by JOB

"The righteousness of the perfect shall direct his way: but the wicked shall fall by his own wickedness."

PROVERBS

"Sin no more, lest a worse thing come unto thee."

CHRIST JESUS
As Recorded by JOHN

"Judge not, that ye be not judged.
For with what judgment ye judge, ye shall be judged: and with what measure ye mete, it shall be measured to you again."

CHRIST JESUS
As Recorded by MATTHEW

Karmic law functions in your life when you accept the belief that you are a descendant of Adam and Eve. Under this law of Karma, there is a reward for every good deed that you perform and a punishment for every sin that you commit. But it is not God who punishes you for your sins. Any punishment that you receive is a result of Karmic law in action.

However, both the rewards and punishments meted out by this so-called law exist only in that spurious physical realm which Jesus referred to as "this world." When you "live, move, and have your being" in "My kingdom"—the fourth dimensional realm of spiritual reality—you rise above the laws of cause and effect, and Karmic law no longer functions in your experience.

The Apostle Paul realized that, as a human being, he not only was subject to the laws of "this world" but, also, was utterly incapable of controlling his own actions:

"For that which I do I allow not: for what I would, that do I not; but what I hate, that do I.

If then I do that which I would not, I consent unto the law that it is good.

Now then it is no more I that do it, but sin that dwelleth in me.

For I know that in me (that is, in my flesh,) dwelleth no good thing: for to will is present with me; but how to perform that which is good I find not.

For the good that I would I do not: but the evil which I would not, that I do.

Now if I do that I would not, it is no more I that do it, but sin that dwelleth in me.

I find then a law, that, when I would do good, evil is present with me.

For I delight in the law of God after the inward man:

But I see another law in my members, warring against the law of my mind, and bringing me into captivity to the law of sin which is in my members.

O wretched man that I am! Who shall deliver me from the body of this death?"

PAUL
To The ROMANS

Even the enlightened apostle had difficulty in reconciling his inward desire to do good with the outward actions of his humanhood. Paul knew that his real identity, the Christ within him, wanted to do the will of the Father. But he also realized that that part of him which was functioning as the "natural man" was not capable of showing forth spiritual perfection: "The good that I would, I do not: but the evil which I would not, that I do."

But then this apostle to the Gentiles discerned the most important truth of all: "Now if I do that I would not, it is no more I that do it, but sin that dwelleth in me."

Paul is telling us that evil does not have its origin in us but is an impersonal suggestion that initially appears in our mind as a temptation, enticing us to accept an identity segregated and removed from God-Consciousness. Then, if we succumb to that suggestion, this false concept of life begins to operate *in, as,* and *through* us.

However, the Divine *I* within each of us—that spiritual essence which is our true identity—is, in fact, the individualized expression of God's Being and, therefore, can only do the works of the Father: "My Father worketh hitherto, and *I* work." But when we accept a selfhood apart from God—when we believe that the issues of our life are dependent upon the functions of a physical body—we are living as the "natural man" and, in that state, are subject to all the laws of "this world." Among these is the law of Karma, which operates in our experience when we allow ourself to be disconnected from the universal "tree of life." Under Karmic law we will be faced with any number of evil circumstances and conditions. But we have the inherent ability to see through these appearances and to rise above them.

The first step in seeing through these situations is to realize that evil was not created by God and does not even exist in the Divine Consciousness. It then follows that any evil appearing in our experience is an illusion and is manifesting itself in our mind as an impersonal temptation which is trying to seduce us into accepting a presence and power other than God.

"Let no man say when he is tempted, 'I am tempted of God:' for God cannot be tempted with evil, neither tempteth He any man."

JAMES

"Then was Jesus led up of the Spirit into the wilderness to be tempted of the devil.

And when he had fasted forty days and forty nights, he was afterward an hungered.

And when the tempter came to him, he said, 'If thou be the Son of God, command that these stones be made bread.'

But [Jesus] answered and said, 'It is written, Man shall not live by bread alone, but by every word that proceedeth out of the mouth of God.'

Then the devil taketh him up into the holy city, and setteth him on a pinnacle of the temple,

And saith unto him, 'If thou be the Son of God, cast thyself down: for it is written, He shall give His angels charge concerning thee: and in their hands they shall bear thee up, lest at any time thou dash thy foot against a stone.'

Jesus said unto him, 'It is written again, Thou shalt not tempt the Lord thy God.'

Again, the devil taketh him up into an exceeding high mountain, and sheweth him all the kingdoms of the world, and the glory of them;

And saith unto him, 'All these things will I give thee, if thou wilt fall down and worship me.'

Then saith Jesus unto him, 'Get thee hence, Satan: for it is written, Thou shalt worship the Lord thy God, and Him only shalt thou serve.'"

MATTHEW

"Ye are of your father the devil, and the lusts of your father ye will do. He was a murderer from the beginning, and abode not in the truth, because there is no truth in him. When he speaketh a lie, he speaketh of his own: for he is a liar, and the father of it."

CHRIST JESUS
As Recorded by JOHN

By refusing to accept the temptations that came to him in the wilderness, Christ Jesus set the standard for all time and truly established himself as the Wayshower.

Similarly, we have the capacity to follow the Master's perceptive example by realizing that all the evil circumstances and conditions that appear in our life also are nothing more than temptations—temptations which lure us into believing that we have a selfhood or identity that is alienated from its Source. If we accept this claim of a personal selfhood, we then become subject to all the limitations that inevitably follow. Our human sense of existence is fraught with fears, doubts and concerns, all of which are predicated upon an erroneous premise. But our real, and only, life-experience does not take place in the physical world of cause and effect. We exist eternally in a fourth-dimensional reality of Divine Being. Our true identity is *I*, the Christ, and this *I* is functioning in a spiritual realm which transcends the pairs of opposites.

Therefore, in order for us to experience the perfection of our divine *I*-dentity, we need to see through the false pictures of material sense. As we develop this clear perspective, we find that we are reacting less to the discordant circumstances that come into our life, and we no longer attempt to do battle with every evil appearance. Functioning at that enlightened level of consciousness, we can more readily comply with the Master's profound injunctions:

"But I say unto you, That ye resist not evil:
Put up again thy sword into his place: for all they that take the sword shall perish with the sword."

CHRIST JESUS
As Recorded by MATTHEW

"Ye shall not need to fight in this battle: set yourselves, stand ye still, and see the salvation of the Lord with you."

2nd CHRONICLES

"Be strong and courageous, be not afraid nor dismayed for the king of Assyria, nor for all the multitude that is with him: for there be more with us than with him:
With him is an arm of flesh; but with us is the Lord our God . . . And the people rested themselves upon [those] words."

HEZEKIAH, King of Judah
As Recorded in 2nd CHRONICLES

Evil must be recognized for what it is: "the arm of flesh," or nothingness. When we resist evil, we give it power and make it seem like a reality. But the secret of true mystical living is to "stand ye still" at the onset of any discordant appearances and to realize that these are only temptations coming to us. Initially these temptations come to our mind as mere suggestions, but if we personalize them, if we accept them as being actual conditions, they will function hypnotically in our experience and, very quickly, will have us believing that they have the power to affect our life.

As the perfect expression of Divine Principle, we live in the pure domain of God-Consciousness. In this "kingdom of God," there is nothing of an evil nature. The ever-present allness of good acts as a law of elimination to anything unlike itself.

Therefore, when we are faced with any evil circumstance, we must know the truth that the Life that is God is forever expressing Itself as our individual life. Hence, our life is eternal and cannot be affected by any temporary form of inharmony. In that illumined state of awareness, we do not resist evil, but we recognize every negative appearance as nothing more than a temptation for us to accept the belief in two powers. Instead of tasting the fruit of the tree of the knowledge of good and evil, we rise above these pairs of opposites by acknowledging that only good is real. But we also understand that this reality is not merely a temporary, human sense of good, but actually is the true state of transcendental spiritual wholeness that is our divine birthright.

The creation narrative in the first chapter of Genesis tells us that "God saw everything that He had made, and, behold, it was very good." As we meditate on this fundamental premise, it will become a vital and living aspect of our consciousness. This, in turn, will help us to discard our false sense of self and will allow the Spirit of God which dwells in the depths of our soul to come forth and fulfill Itself *through* and *as* our life.

"Be not overcome of evil, but overcome evil with good."

PAUL
To the ROMANS

"'Not by might, nor by power, but by My Spirit,' saith the Lord of hosts."

ZECHARIAH

LOVE
("God Is Love")

"And thou shalt love the Lord thy God with all thine heart, and with all thy soul, and with all thy might."

MOSES
As Recorded in DEUTERONOMY

"Thou shalt love thy neighbour as thyself."

CHRIST JESUS
As Recorded by MARK

When Jesus was asked: "Which is the first commandment?" he quoted the Old Testament directive to love God with all our heart, soul and mind, and then he added the command to "love [our] neighbour as [ourself]." But is it possible to follow these dictates of the Master? Is it possible to love God with every fiber of our being?

Consider all those people who, through the ages, have accepted the old theological teachings which describe their God as a God of wrath and vengeance; a Ruler who judges and condemns; a Potentate who rewards and punishes; a First Cause who not only is aware of evil but, according to world belief, is the very creator of evil.

How could such a God be the object of our affection? How could anyone love such a false concept of Deity?

Fortunately, those of us on the spiritual path have not been asked to make such a difficult commitment. We are not expected to love the "Lord God" of the Old Testament.

Mystical Truth has revealed that God is infinite Consciousness, the only Life-Force that exists. Since this Divine Being, then, unfolds and expresses Itself as All that Is, everything comprising God's realm of spiritual reality must be perfect and complete. The infallible Divine Consciousness has not created anything that is separate from, nor antagonistic to, Its own immaculate Self-expression.

"And God saw everything that He had made, and, behold, it was very good."

GENESIS

Since everything that exists in God-Consciousness has been pronounced "very good," there really are no pairs of opposites. There cannot be good and evil, cause and effect, or action and reaction; only the one-way flow of pure Being revealing and disclosing Itself in all of Its consummate perfection—no judgment, no condemnation, no rewards and no punishment.

The spiritually inspired apostle John gave us the ultimate description of God:

"God is Love."

1st Epistle of JOHN

The Love that is God is omnipresent, and this Divine Love perpetually flows out from the Source, unfolding as perfect harmony. But Divine Love is unconditional and universal; it does not seek a reciprocal response; it has no object. Therefore, each one of us, as the individualized manifestation of God's Being, is foreordained to be under the influence and receive the benefit of this perfect Love. "[God] maketh His sun to rise on the evil and on the good, and sendeth rain on the just and on the unjust." But, in order for us to become a pure transparency through which this omnipresent Divine Love can be expressed, we must achieve a mystical awareness of Truth and comply with certain spiritual precepts:

"If we love one another, God dwelleth in us, and His love is perfected in us."

1st Epistle of JOHN

"This is my commandment, That ye love one another, as I have loved you."

CHRIST JESUS
As Recorded by JOHN

"Freely ye have received, freely give."

CHRIST JESUS
As Recorded by MATTHEW

The perfect Love of God is always with us, pouring through us into active expression. But in order for that Love to be evident in our visible experience, we must become a willing channel for that divine attribute, allowing It to flow out into the world.

Our love for our fellow man testifies to our love for God.

"If a man say, "I love God," and hateth his brother, he is a liar: for he that loveth not his brother whom he hath seen, how can he love God whom he hath not seen?

And this commandment have we from Him, that he who loveth God love his brother also."

1st Epistle of JOHN

"Though I speak with the tongues of men and of angels, and have not [love], I am become as sounding brass, or a tinkling cymbal.

And though I have the gift of prophecy, and understand all mysteries, and all knowledge; and though I have all faith, so that I could remove mountains, and have not [love], I am nothing.

And though I bestow all my goods to feed the poor, and though I give my body to be burned, and have not [love], it profiteth me nothing.

[Love] never faileth: but whether there be prophecies, they shall fail; whether there be tongues, they shall cease; whether there be knowledge, it shall vanish away.

And now abideth faith, hope, [love], these three; but the greatest of these is [love]."

PAUL
To the CORINTHIANS

"Owe no man any thing, but to love one another: for he that loveth another hath fulfilled the law."

PAUL
To the ROMANS

Some of the most basic principles of spiritual living were given to us by the Master in his remarkable discourse "The Sermon on the Mount." The degree to which our love must be expressed is fully presented in that treatise:

"Blessed are the poor in spirit: for theirs is the Kingdom of heaven.

Blessed are they that mourn: for they shall be comforted.

Blessed are the meek: for they shall inherit the earth.

Blessed are they which do hunger and thirst after righteousness: for they shall be filled.

Blessed are the merciful: for they shall obtain mercy.

Blessed are the pure in heart: for they shall see God.

Blessed are the peacemakers: for they shall be called the children of God.

Blessed are they which are persecuted for righteousness' sake: for theirs is the Kingdom of heaven.

Blessed are ye, when men shall revile you, and persecute you, and shall say all manner of evil against you falsely, for my sake.

Rejoice, and be exceeding glad: for great is your reward in heaven: for so persecuted they the prophets which were before you.

Ye are the light of the world. A city that is set on an hill cannot be hid.

Neither do men light a candle, and put it under a bushel, but on a candlestick; and it giveth light unto all that are in the house.

Let your light so shine before men, that they may see your good works, and glorify your Father which is in heaven.

Ye have heard that it hath been said, An eye for an eye, and a tooth for a tooth:

But I say unto you, That ye resist not evil: but whosoever shall smite thee on thy right cheek, turn to him the other also.

And if any man will sue thee at the law, and take away thy coat, let him have thy cloak also.

And whosoever shall compel thee to go a mile, go with him twain.

Give to him that asketh thee, and from him that would borrow of thee turn not thou away.

Ye have heard that it hath been said, Thou shalt love thy neighbour, and hate thine enemy.

But I say unto you, Love your enemies, bless them that curse you, do good to them that hate you, and pray for them which despitefully use you, and persecute you;

That ye may be the children of your Father which is in heaven...

For if ye love them which love you, what reward have ye? Do not even the publicans the same?

And if ye salute your brethren only, what do ye more than others? Do not even the publicans so?

Be ye therefore perfect, even as your Father which is in heaven is perfect."

CHRIST JESUS
As Recorded by MATTHEW

The rules for living which are outlined in the "Sermon On the Mount" appear to be quite radical and, in actual practice, may seem very difficult to live up to. Yet, if we wish to develop a spiritually enlightened consciousness, we must adhere to these commands. The inner mystical life is aided greatly when our outer experience conforms to these high standards.

As we continue to dwell in that kingdom at the center of our soul, we become less concerned about the external circumstances of our life and also find it easier to live according to the code of love outlined by Jesus. But the Master has given us some further instructions which take us to an even higher level of mystical living. Following these directives with a willing heart will assuredly make us a pure instrument of Divine Love:

"Give to every man that asketh of thee; and of him that taketh away thy goods ask them not again.

And as ye would that men should do to you, do ye also to them likewise."

CHRIST JESUS
As Recorded by LUKE

"Greater love hath no man than this, that a man lay down his life for his friends."

CHRIST JESUS
As Recorded by JOHN

If we are capable of following these most important commands of the Master, we will become a transparency through which the Love and Life of God will be visibly expressed; and, conversely, only when Divine Love is active in us are we capable of adhering to these lofty precepts. Then, functioning under this grace of God, we truly will be living the mystical life.

"Love not the world, neither the things that are in the world. If any man love the world, the love of the Father is not in him.

Ye are of God, little children, and have overcome them: because greater is He that is in you, than he that is in the world.

Beloved, let us love one another: for love is of God; and every one that loveth is born of God, and knoweth God.

He that loveth not knoweth not God; for God is Love.

There is no fear in love; but perfect love casteth out fear... He that feareth is not made perfect in love.

Herein is love, not that we loved God, but that he loved us...

Beloved, if God so loved us, we ought to love one another...

Hereby know we that we dwell in Him, and He in us, because He hath given us of His Spirit.

Behold, what manner of love the Father hath bestowed upon us, that we should be called the sons of God: therefore the world knoweth us not, because it knew Him not.

Beloved, now are we the sons of God, and it doth not yet appear what we shall be: but we know that, when He shall appear, we shall be like Him; for we shall see Him as He is.

And every man that hath this hope in him purifieth himself, even as He is pure."

1st Epistle of JOHN

PRAYER
(Meditation and Communion)

"Pray without ceasing."

> PAUL
> To the THESSALONIANS

"Let the words of my mouth, and the meditation of my heart, be acceptable in Thy sight, O Lord."

> PSALM 19

"The effectual, fervent prayer of a righteous man availeth much."

> JAMES

"Now faith is the substance of things hoped for, the evidence of things not seen."

> HEBREWS

Ever since some prehistoric human being realized that there must be a First Cause, or Creator, of the universe, mankind has been trying to establish a relationship with this Supreme Being.

As the human race developed intellectually, many different concepts of God evolved, and each new concept produced its own forms of worship and prayer. Seeking to rise above the limitations of his humanhood, the "man of earth" used every means at his disposal to try to influence his God.

Ultimately, the light of Truth began to dawn in human consciousness, and a few enlightened souls turned within themselves in contemplation. There they discovered a hidden Presence, a higher sense of Self. But at first this inner Presence was misunderstood, and people continued looking to a God outside of their own being. Based on that erroneous premise, the earliest attempts at contact with God were carried out through rituals of sacrifice, and an intrinsic aspect of these rituals was the prayer of petition.

In those so-called prayers, it became an accepted practice to ask God to fulfill man's personal desires. The Divine Principle of the universe—"the Father of lights, with whom is no variableness, neither shadow of turning"—was regarded as a servant who could be used by mortals to do their bidding.

What a limited, false concept of Deity!

God is infinite Consciousness; the only Life, Substance and Intelligence. This omnipresent Being is All-in-all. Nothing exists external to God-Consciousness, and all that exists therein is God's own perception and unfoldment of Itself.

Therefore, the first and most basic step in true prayer is to acknowledge the infinite nature of God. We must consciously realize that "greater is He that is in [us] than he that is in the world" and, then, we must surrender ourself to that Divine Presence, allowing It to take over every aspect of our life.

"Trust in the Lord with all thine heart; and lean not unto thine own understanding.

In all thy ways acknowledge Him, and He shall direct thy paths."

PROVERBS

"*Acquaint now thyself with Him, and be at peace: thereby good shall come unto thee.*"

ELIPHAZ, the Temanite
As Recorded by JOB

"*Thou wilt keep him in perfect peace, whose mind is stayed on Thee: because he trusteth in Thee.*

'*For My thoughts are not your thoughts, neither are your ways My ways,*' *saith the Lord.*

'*For as the heavens are higher than the earth, so are My ways higher than your ways, and My thoughts than your thoughts.*

'*So shall My word be that goeth forth out of My mouth: it shall not return unto Me void, but it shall accomplish that which I please, and it shall prosper in the thing whereto I sent it.*'"

ISAIAH

"*For we know not what we should pray for as we ought: but the Spirit Itself maketh intercession for us with groanings which cannot be uttered.*

And he that searcheth the hearts knoweth what is the mind of the Spirit...

For we know that all things work together for good to them that love God, to them who are the called according to His purpose."

PAUL
To the ROMANS

After we have acknowledged the ever-present allness of God, we must be willing to "trust in the Lord with all [our] heart."

The truth of Being is eternally established. God is infinite Consciousness, and nothing exists outside of this omniscient Intelligence. We cannot inform the All-knowing Divine Wisdom of anything that It does not already apprehend. For that reason, prayers which attempt to influence God are of no benefit.

"Ask, and it shall be given you; seek, and ye shall find; knock, and it shall be opened unto you."

CHRIST JESUS
As Recorded by MATTHEW

"Ye ask, and receive not, because ye ask amiss, that ye may consume it upon your lusts."

JAMES

Realizing that their prayers of petition have very seldom, if ever, been answered, discerning men and women have diligently sought a higher form of prayer. As these people gained a greater awareness of spiritual reality, they recognized the futility of asking the Divine Principle of the universe to change anything in Its already perfect creation. Ultimate reality, or the "kingdom of God," was established in the beginning. Accordingly, man's only task is to bring himself into harmony with this absolute perfection.

Out of this realization, another form of prayer evolved: the prayer of affirmation. In these prayers, man did not ask God for anything but, rather, by stating and restating the facts of being, man tried to mentally convince himself of his relationship to Deity.

While this concept of prayer, certainly, was more logical than the earlier sacrifices and petitions, many people misunderstood the purpose of affirmations and began using them as an "end" rather than as a "means to an end." In some cases, these prayers of affirmation almost degenerated to the level of the "vain repetitions" which were condemned by Jesus:

"But when ye pray, use not vain repetitions, as the heathen do: for they think that they shall be heard for their much speaking."

CHRIST JESUS
As Recorded by MATTHEW

The ultimate form of prayer, then, is one in which we bring ourself into harmony with the spiritual reality that already exists in Divine Consciousness. But this cannot be done while we are functioning in this conceptual world or while we are thinking worldly thoughts. Isaiah tells us, "Thou wilt keep him in perfect peace, whose mind is stayed on Thee."

"Keeping our mind stayed on God" is an activity which begins with an acknowledgement that we don't know our real needs, but the "Father [Who] dwelleth in [us]" does. Then we must surrender all of our human opinions, desires and fears, and seek to learn the will of this Father within.

"Nevertheless, not my will, but Thine, be done."

CHRIST JESUS
As Recorded by LUKE

"Therefore, I say unto you, Take no thought for your life, what ye shall eat, or what ye shall drink; nor yet for your body, what ye shall put on. Is not life more than meat, and the body than raiment?

Which of you by taking thought can add one cubit unto his stature?

Therefore, take no thought, saying, 'What shall we eat?' or, 'Wherewithal shall we be clothed?'

But seek ye first the kingdom of God, and His righteousness; and all these things shall be added unto you."

CHRIST JESUS
As Recorded by MATTHEW

In one of his highest teachings, the Master Christian has told us to "seek. . .the kingdom of God, and His righteousness." Since this kingdom exists in the silent sanctuary of our own soul, we can achieve true prayer only when we turn within ourself in contemplation and meditation.

"And when thou prayest, thou shalt not be as the hypocrites are: for they love to pray standing in the synagogues and in the corners of the streets, that they may be seen of men. Verily I say unto you, they have their reward.

But thou, when thou prayest, enter into thy closet, and when thou hast shut thy door, pray to thy Father which is in secret; and thy Father which seeth in secret shall reward thee openly."

CHRIST JESUS
As Recorded by MATTHEW

This closet that the Master commanded us to enter is, in fact, the inner chamber of our own being. It is there that we seek a mystical union with the Divine Consciousness, and it is only in that union that we achieve true prayer. But in order for us to make this contact with God, we must take certain steps which will prepare ourself for such an experience. We must approach our meditations with a proper attitude, and this, in turn, helps to create an atmosphere of receptivity.

"Therefore, if thou bring thy gift to the altar, and there rememberest that thy brother hath ought against thee;
Leave there thy gift before the altar and go thy way; first be reconciled to thy brother, and then come and offer thy gift."

CHRIST JESUS
As Recorded by MATTHEW

"For verily I say unto you, that whosoever shall say unto this mountain, 'Be thou removed, and be thou cast into the sea;' and shall not doubt in his heart, but shall believe that those things which he saith shall come to pass, he shall have whatsoever he saith.
Therefore, I say unto you, What things soever ye desire, when ye pray, believe that ye receive them, and ye shall have them.
And when ye stand praying, forgive, if ye have ought against any: that your Father also which is in heaven may forgive your trespasses."

CHRIST JESUS
As Recorded by MARK

The Apostle Paul told us that "the natural man receiveth not the things of God." Therefore, in order for us to make contact with God—in order for us to have a true God-experience—we must rise above our "natural man" state of existence.

This principle was further confirmed by Christ Jesus when he instructed us not to approach the altar of God while we "have ought against our brother." If we are holding anyone in condemnation, we still are functioning as the "man of earth" and, in that state, are alienated from God-Consciousness. So it follows that our first step in returning to the "Father's household" is to "forgive those who have trespassed against us" and to hold no one in bondage for his past sins of omission or commission.

"Neither do I condemn thee: go, and sin no more."

CHRIST JESUS
As Recorded by JOHN

"Then came Peter to him, and said, 'Lord, how oft shall my brother sin against me, and I forgive him? till seven times?'

Jesus saith unto him, 'I say not unto thee, Until seven times: but Until seventy times seven.'"

MATTHEW

This act of forgiveness must also be directed to ourself. We must forgive ourself for all of our past mistakes and negative actions. In doing this, we will be rising to a higher level of consciousness—a level at which we can begin to comprehend Paul's profound command:

"Let this mind be in you, which was also in Christ Jesus."

PAUL
To the PHILIPPIANS

"Be ye therefore perfect, even as your Father which is in heaven is perfect."

CHRIST JESUS
As Recorded by MATTHEW

As we gain a clearer recognition of our true identity, we soon realize that we already have that "mind . . . which was also in Christ Jesus." In this Christ-mind, there is no condemnation. The Christ was able to forgive the woman taken in adultery and the thief on the cross. But the Christ-mind has also risen above most of the other human characteristics. In this mind, we find no fear nor doubt, no jealousy, envy, hatred, nor any other negative emotions.

Only as we recognize our Christhood can we truly "be... perfect, even as [our] Father which is in heaven is perfect," and only as the Christ can we achieve a mystical union with God.

Divine Consciousness is cognizant of nothing but Itself: "I AM That I AM." This activity of Consciousness knowing and perceiving Itself constitutes our individual Christ-identity. For this reason, God is not aware of the descendants of Adam and Eve. These "men of earth" exist in a suppositional, three-dimensional realm of cause and effect—a realm that is completely segregated from God-Consciousness. Therefore, if we are among those who have accepted an identity as the "natural man," we must "die" to this false sense of life and, ultimately, must gain a full awareness of our Christ-identity. Functioning from that awakened standpoint, we then can practice the highest form of prayer.

We begin this prayer by contemplating the things of God. We consciously realize all the facts we know about the truth of Being. Then, after a period of this mental activity, we reach a point beyond the thinking process.

At that moment, we have surrendered all of our limited human characteristics. We are "resting in the Word" and are in a meditative state of spiritual receptivity, listening for the Voice of God . . . waiting to feel the Presence of God. . . .

"And behold, the Lord passed by, and a great and strong wind rent the mountains, and brake in pieces the rocks before the Lord; but the Lord was not in the wind: and after the wind an earthquake; but the Lord was not in the earthquake:

And after the earthquake a fire; but the Lord was not in the fire: and after the fire a still small voice."

1st KINGS

"Speak, Lord; for Thy servant heareth."

SAMUEL

As the Divine Presence descends upon us, we achieve a realization that we now are at one with all life. God, the Father and God, the Son are one. This is the ultimate form of prayer. God speaks, and we hear . . . Divine Consciousness reveals Itself *in* and *as* our individual consciousness. God, the Great I AM, appears as *I*, the Christ.

Resting in that perfect state of oneness, we realize that this *I* within us was begotten, not made. As the peace of God fills our Soul, we accept our divine birthright. "*I* and my Father are One". . . *I* am God-incarnate!

"And the peace of God, which passeth all understanding, shall keep your hearts and minds through Christ Jesus."

PAUL
To the PHILIPPIANS

"Peace I leave with you, my peace I give unto you: not as the world giveth, give I unto you."

CHRIST JESUS
As Recorded by JOHN

SPIRITUAL HEALING
(*"By Their Fruits Ye Shall Know Them"*)

"And Jesus went about all Galilee, teaching in their synagogues, and preaching the gospel of the kingdom, and healing all manner of sickness and all manner of disease among the people.

And his fame went throughout all Syria: and they brought unto him all sick people that were taken with divers diseases and torments, and those which were possessed with devils, and those which were lunatick, and those that had the palsy; and he healed them.

And there followed him great multitudes of people from Galilee, and from Decapolis, and from Jerusalem, and from Judea, and from beyond Jordan."

MATTHEW

"And there came a leper to him, beseeching him, and kneeling down to him, and saying unto him, 'If thou wilt, thou canst make me clean.'

And Jesus, moved with compassion, put forth his hand, and touched him, and saith unto him, 'I will; be thou clean.'

And as soon as he had spoken, immediately the leprosy departed from him, and he was cleansed."

MARK

"And behold, men brought in a bed a man which was taken with a palsy: and they sought means to bring him in, and to lay him before him.

And when they could not find by what way they might bring him in because of the multitude, they went upon the housetop, and let him down through the tiling with his couch into the midst before Jesus.

And when he saw their faith, he said unto him, 'Man, thy sins are forgiven thee.'

And the scribes and the Pharisees began to reason, saying, 'Who is this which speaketh blasphemies? Who can forgive sins, but God alone?'

But when Jesus perceived their thoughts, he answering said unto them, 'What reason ye in your hearts?

'Whether is easier, to say, Thy sins be forgiven thee; or to say, Rise up and walk?

'But that ye may know that the Son of man hath power upon earth to forgive sins,' (he said unto the sick of the palsy,) 'I say unto thee, Arise, and take up thy couch, and go into thine house.'

And immediately he rose up before them, and took up that whereon he lay, and departed to his own house, glorifying God."

LUKE

"So Jesus came again into Cana of Galilee, where he made the water wine. And there was a certain nobleman, whose son was sick at Capernaum.

When he heard that Jesus was come out of Judea into Galilee, he went unto him, and besought him that he would come down, and heal his son: for he was at the point of death.

Then said Jesus unto him, 'Except ye see signs and wonders, ye will not believe.'

The nobleman saith unto him, 'Sir, come down ere my child die.'

Jesus saith unto him, 'Go thy way; thy son liveth.' And the man believed the word that Jesus had spoken unto him, and he went his way.

And as he was now going down, his servants met him, and told him, saying, 'Thy son liveth.'

Then enquired he of them the hour when he began to amend. And they said unto him, 'Yesterday at the seventh hour the fever left him.'

So the father knew that it was at the same hour, in the which Jesus said unto him, 'Thy son liveth:' and himself believed, and his whole house."

JOHN

To an uninformed observer, the healing works performed by Christ Jesus might be construed as specific examples of divine intervention in the human scene. Was this an activity in which the "Father of lights, with whom is no variableness" was correcting mistakes in His own creation? Was this a special dispensation in which physical and material laws were set aside?

In truth, these events were performed in perfect consonance with universal principles that still are available today.

If we recognize God as the one omniscient Consciousness, we then must understand that this infinite Being has no knowledge of any false concepts about Itself. Truth can never be aware of error. God knows nothing about a hypothetical physical realm and, for that reason, does not function in the human arena.

How, then, were the seeming miracles of the Bible performed?

Logic dictates that these events were not miracles. They did not negate any real laws, but were visible demonstrations of an inner activity of illumined consciousness.

Jesus had a full awareness of his Christ-identity. He acknowledged and accepted his oneness with God and, in that realization, was able to rise above all personal sense of self.

As his Jesus-mind surrendered itself, his Christ-consciousness could be revealed; and whenever this pure, spiritual state of being is manifested, Its omnipresence functions as a law of elimination to anything unlike Itself.

"[Jesus] saith unto them, 'But whom say ye that I am?'

And Simon Peter answered and said, 'Thou art the Christ, the Son of the Living God."

MATTHEW

"Now when the sun was setting, all they that had any sick with divers diseases brought them unto him, and he laid his hands on every one of them, and healed them.

And devils also came out of many, crying out, and saying, 'Thou art Christ the Son of God.' And he rebuking them suffered them not to speak: for they knew that he was Christ."

LUKE

"*The Spirit of the Lord is upon me, because He hath anointed me to preach the gospel to the poor; He hath sent me to heal the brokenhearted, to preach deliverance to the captives, and recovering of sight to the blind, to set at liberty them that are bruised.*"

Prophecy of ESAIAS
Read by CHRIST JESUS
As Recorded by LUKE

"*And when Jesus was entered into Capernaum, there came unto him a centurion, beseeching him,*

And saying, 'Lord, my servant lieth at home sick of the palsy, grievously tormented.'

And Jesus saith unto him, 'I will come and heal him.'

The centurion answered and said, 'Lord, I am not worthy that thou shouldest come under my roof: but speak the word only, and my servant shall be healed.

'For I am a man under authority, having soldiers under me: and I say to this man, Go, and he goeth; and to another, Come, and he cometh; and to my servant, Do this, and he doeth it.'

When Jesus heard it, he marvelled, and said to them that followed, 'Verily I say unto you, I have not found so great faith, no, not in Israel.'

And Jesus said unto the centurion, 'Go thy way; and as thou hast believed, so be it done unto thee.' And his servant was healed in the selfsame hour."

MATTHEW

"*And Jesus went with him; and much people followed him and thronged him.*

And a certain woman, which had an issue of blood twelve years,

And had suffered many things of many physicians, and had spent all that she had, and was nothing bettered, but rather grew worse,

When she had heard of Jesus, came in the press behind, and touched his garment.

For she said, 'If I may touch but his clothes, I shall be whole.'

And straightway the fountain of her blood was dried up; and she felt in her body that she was healed of that plague.

And Jesus, immediately knowing in himself that virtue had gone out of him, turned him about in the press, and said, 'Who touched my clothes?'

And his disciples said unto him, 'Thou seest the multitude thronging thee, and sayest thou, 'Who touched me?'

And he looked round about to see her that had done this thing.

But the woman fearing and trembling, knowing what was done in her, came and fell down before him, and told him all the truth.

And he said unto her, 'Daughter, thy faith hath made thee whole; go in peace, and be whole of thy plague.'"

MARK

In the Biblical accounts of Jesus' healing ministry, the Master is often reputed as making statements such as: "Thy faith hath made thee whole" and "As thou hast believed, so be it done unto thee."

Reading those words today, we might interpret them as implying that, perhaps, blind faith is a factor in the healing process. This is not necessarily the case. Many of the words used by the Master in his original Aramaic language had a much broader meaning than that which can be derived from the words appearing in our present-day Scriptural translations.

Faith and belief are activities of the human mind. But this human-sense-of-mind virtually plays no part in spiritual healing. A true spiritual healing, as demonstrated by Christ Jesus, is brought about when an enlightened person achieves a mystical union with the Divine Consciousness. In that union, the finite human mind ceases to function of its own accord and, instead, becomes a transparency through which God-Consciousness can reveal Itself. This revelation of Divine Being then operates as a law of adjustment to any erroneous circumstances or conditions that may be appearing at our present level of perception.

"And when Jesus departed thence, two blind men followed him, crying, and saying, 'Thou son of David, have mercy on us.'

And when he was come into the house, the blind men came to him: and Jesus saith unto them, 'Believe ye that I am able to do this?' They said unto him, 'Yea, Lord.'

Then touched he their eyes, saying, 'According to your faith be it unto you.'

And their eyes were opened; and Jesus straitly charged them, saying, 'See that no man know it.'

But they, when they were departed, spread abroad his fame in all that country."

MATTHEW

"And [Jesus] arose out of the synagogue, and entered into Simon's house. And Simon's wife's mother was taken with a great fever; and they besought him for her.

And he stood over her, and rebuked the fever; and it left her: and immediately she arose and ministered unto them."

LUKE

"And it came to pass after these things, that the son of the woman, the mistress of the house, fell sick; and his sickness was so sore, that there was no breath left in him.

And she said unto Elijah, 'What have I to do with thee, O thou man of God? Art thou come unto me to call my sin to remembrance, and to slay my son?'

And he said unto her, 'Give me thy son.' And he took him out of her bosom, and carried him up into a loft, where he abode, and laid him upon his own bed.

And he cried unto the Lord, and said, 'O Lord my God, hast thou also brought evil upon the widow with whom I sojourn, by slaying her son?'

And he stretched himself upon the child three times, and cried unto the Lord, and said, 'O Lord my God, I pray thee, let this child's soul come into him again.'

And the Lord heard the voice of Elijah; and the soul of the child came into him again, and he revived.

And Elijah took the child, and brought him down out of the chamber into the house, and delivered him unto his mother: and Elijah said, 'See, thy son liveth.'

And the woman said to Elijah, 'Now by this I know that thou art a man of God, and that the word of the Lord in thy mouth is truth.'"

1st KINGS

"Ye shall know the truth, and the truth shall make you free."

CHRIST JESUS
As Recorded by JOHN

Most of the healings and other purported miracles recorded in the Old Testament imply that some specially anointed holy person was capable of uttering prayers or making supplications to God—prayers which could actually influence the Supreme Being to change or correct circumstances and conditions in the three-dimensional, physical universe.

This is an extremely illogical and contradictory approach to Deity! Surely, we cannot believe that a limited and finite human mind could possibly inform the omniscient Divine Consciousness of anything, because in that same Bible we read:

"O the depth of the riches both of the wisdom and knowledge of God! How unsearchable are His judgements, and His ways past finding out!"

PAUL
To the ROMANS

"His understanding is infinite."

PSALM 147

In the New Testament descriptions of Jesus' healing ministry, we never hear of him asking God to cure anyone. The Master's promise is: "Ye shall know the truth, and the truth shall make you free."

What is this truth that, when fully comprehended, will give us our freedom from the discords of this world?

It is the most basic premise of all mystical teachings. This premise reveals that God is the only Life, Substance, and Intelligence—the one infinite Consciousness. And because this Universal Consciousness is expressing and revealing Itself as our individual consciousness, we must exhibit all the characteristics of the Godhead.

God's Being is perfect. Therefore, God's individualized manifestation (our true spiritual identity) must display that same perfection. That is why any diseases, any lacks, or any other problems occurring in our experience must be mentally reinterpreted and recognized as illusions—as temptations appearing in our mind.

This reinterpretation process is the first step in spiritual healing. Otherwise, if we entertain and accept these suggestions, they begin to act hypnotically upon us and, very quickly, have us believing that we have a selfhood separated from God-Consciousness; that our life is dependent upon the functions of a physical body; and that these erroneous appearances are something real and tangible. These false claims, which originally appeared to us as impersonal temptations, then become personalized and begin to manifest themselves externally in our experience as visible forms and effects, i.e., physical and mental diseases, financial lacks, problems in human relationships, and a myriad of other negative circumstances. But as is the case with any form of hypnotism, the person being influenced by mental suggestions must be awakened from the hypnotic spell. All the events that are allegedly taking place under the hypnosis are not real and, therefore, cannot be cured or changed if we accept them at face value—as actually being what they purport themselves to be.

Similarly, when we function as "the man of earth," we are living in the "Adam dream" which, itself, is a subtle form of hypnotism. Consequently, all the phenomena of this material world—all the circumstances and events that are evident to our physical senses—are not real. For that reason, we cannot change a bad human situation into a good human situation by dealing with it as though it were a constituent of veritable reality.

In other words, never try to meet a problem at the level of the problem!

When you are faced with any adversity in your life, realize that you have the God-endowed capacity to discern the truth about the situation. You can descry the nothingness of this appearance and rise to a higher, spiritual plane of consciousness.

Healing is revealing! Allow the spiritual Son of God— the Christ which you really are—to reveal Itself at the center of your being. That revelation of true identity, then, will function as the restoration of harmony to any discordant appearances that have been presented to you. Always remember that you have no power to heal anything! But when you contact the Christ within you, It can operate through you and will go before you to "make the crooked places straight."

"And when [Jesus] was departed thence, he went into their synagogue:

And, behold, there was a man which had his hand withered. And they asked him, saying, 'Is it lawful to heal on the sabbath days?' that they might accuse him.

And he said unto them, 'What man shall there be among you, that shall have one sheep, and if it fall into a pit on the sabbath day, will he not lay hold on it, and lift it out?

'How much then is a man better than a sheep? Wherefore it is lawful to do well on the sabbath days.'

Then saith he to the man, 'Stretch forth thine hand.' And he stretched it forth; and it was restored whole, like as the other."

MATTHEW

"When the men were come unto [Jesus], they said, 'John Baptist hath sent us unto thee, saying, Art thou he that should come? or look we for another?'

And in that same hour he cured many of their infirmities and plagues, and of evil spirits; and unto many that were blind he gave sight.

Then Jesus answering said unto them, 'Go your way, and tell John what things ye have seen and heard; how that the blind see, the lame walk, the lepers are cleansed, the deaf hear, the dead are raised, to the poor the gospel is preached.'"

LUKE

"And as Jesus passed by, he saw a man which was blind from his birth.

And his disciples asked him, saying, 'Master, who did sin, this man, or his parents, that he was born blind?'

Jesus answered, 'Neither hath this man sinned, nor his parents: but that the works of God should be made manifest in him.

'I must work the works of Him that sent me, while it is day: the night cometh, when no man can work.

'As long as I am in the world, I am the light of the world.'

When he had thus spoken, he spat on the ground, and made clay of the spittle, and he anointed the eyes of the blind man with the clay,

And said unto him, 'Go, wash in the pool of Siloam,' (which is by interpretation, Sent.) He went his way therefore, and washed, and came seeing."

JOHN

Before he healed the man who was blind from birth, Jesus was asked: "Who did sin, this man, or his parents, that he was born blind?"

His reply was: "Neither hath this man sinned, nor his parents."

In giving that answer, the Master disclosed the fundamental truth that neither sickness, nor physical handicaps, nor any other adversities occurring in our lives are inflicted upon us by God as punishment for our sins.

The Infinite Invisible did not create a three-dimensional, material universe and, thus, is not even aware of the conjectural activities supposedly taking place in the human scene. "This world" is nothing more than a false concept of God's real and harmonious creation—a creation that actually is the spiritual unfoldment of pure Being discerning and revealing Its own consummate perfection.

Therefore, the only sin for which we can be punished is mankind's "original sin" of accepting the belief in good and evil.

But it is not God who punishes us for this!

The belief in two powers is merely an impersonal universal claim—an insidious allegation that there is a hypothetical opposite to the allness of infinite Consciousness. Yet, if we, through spiritual ignorance, accept this false claim, we negligently forsake our divine birthright and, thereafter, function as the "natural man." As a result of this ostensible fall from grace, we then become subject to all the laws of "this world," and it is our unmindful acquiescence to these counterfeit laws that is the cause of all our human suffering.

"And, behold, there was a woman which had a spirit of infirmity eighteen years, and was bowed together, and could in no wise lift up herself.

And when Jesus saw her, he called her to him, and said unto her, 'Woman, thou art loosed from thine infirmity.'

And he laid his hands on her: and immediately she was made straight, and glorified God."

LUKE

"And they came to Jericho: and as [Jesus] went out of Jericho with his disciples and a great number of people, blind Bartimaeus, the son of Timaeus, sat by the highway side begging.

And when he heard that it was Jesus of Nazareth, he began to cry out, and say, 'Jesus, thou son of David, have mercy on me.'

And Jesus stood still, and commanded him to be called. And they call the blind man, saying unto him, 'Be of good comfort, rise; he calleth thee.'

And he, casting away his garment, rose, and came to Jesus.

And Jesus answered and said unto him, 'What wilt thou that I should do unto thee?' The blind man said unto him, 'Lord, that I might receive my sight.'

And Jesus said unto him, 'Go thy way; thy faith hath made thee whole.' And immediately he received his sight, and followed Jesus in the way."

MARK

"And it came to pass, as [Jesus] went into the house of one of the chief Pharisees to eat bread on the sabbath day, that they watched him.

And, behold, there was a certain man before him which had the dropsy.

And Jesus answering spake unto the lawyers and Pharisees, saying, 'Is it lawful to heal on the sabbath day?'

And they held their peace. And he took him, and healed him, and let him go."

LUKE

After this there was a feast of the Jews; and Jesus went up to Jerusalem.

Now there is at Jerusalem by the sheep market a pool, which is called in the Hebrew tongue Bethesda, having five porches.

In these lay a great multitude of impotent folk, of blind, halt, withered, waiting for the moving of the water.

For an angel went down at a certain season into the pool, and troubled the water: whosoever then first after the troubling of the water stepped in was made whole of whatsoever disease he had.

And a certain man was there, which had an infirmity thirty and eight years.

When Jesus saw him lie, and knew that he had been now a long time in that case, he saith unto him, 'Wilt thou be made whole?'

The impotent man answered him, 'Sir, I have no man, when the water is troubled, to put me into the pool: but while I am coming, another steppeth down before me.'

Jesus saith unto him, 'Rise, take up thy bed, and walk.'

And immediately the man was made whole, and took up his bed, and walked: and on the same day was the sabbath."

JOHN

As Divine Consciousness individually expresses and reveals Itself, God the Father incarnates and appears as God the Son. This is the real meaning of the immaculate conception and the virgin birth. The result of this activity of Consciousness unfolding, then, is that the Word is made flesh. Christ, the immortal Son of God—the divine ideal of God's own perfect revelation of Itself—dwells among us.

Always remember that any appearance of inharmony or disease is an illusion. Yet in reality, an illusion can never be externalized or objectified. That is why we, too, can overcome all of our seeming problems by awakening to this Christ-Presence within us.

"Thomas saith unto him, 'Lord, we know not whither thou goest; and how can we know the way?'

Jesus saith unto him, 'I am the way, the truth, and the life: no man cometh unto the Father, but by me.

'If ye had known me, ye should have known my Father also: and from henceforth ye know Him, and have seen Him.

'Believest thou not that I am in the Father, and the Father in me? The words that I speak unto you I speak not of myself: but the Father that dwelleth in me, He doeth the works.

'Believe me that I am in the Father, and the Father in me: or else believe me for the very works' sake.

'Verily, verily, I say unto you, He that believeth on me [He that understands my message], the works that I do shall he do also; and greater works than these shall he do; because I go unto my Father.'"

CHRIST JESUS
As Recorded by JOHN

"And [Jesus] called unto him the twelve, and began to send them forth by two and two; and gave them power over unclean spirits;

And commanded them that they should take nothing for their journey, save a staff only; no scrip, no bread, no money in their purse:

And they went out, and preached that men should repent.

And they cast out many devils, and anointed with oil many that were sick, and healed them."

MARK

"Now Peter and John went up together into the temple at the hour of prayer, being the ninth hour.

And a certain man lame from his mother's womb was carried, whom they laid daily at the gate of the temple which is called Beautiful, to ask alms of them that entered into the temple;

Who seeing Peter and John about to go into the temple asked an alms.

And Peter fastening his eyes upon him with John, said, 'Look on us.'

And he gave heed unto them, expecting to receive something of them.

Then Peter said, 'Silver and gold have I none; but such as I have give I thee: In the name of Jesus Christ of Nazareth rise up and walk.'

And he took him by the right hand, and lifted him up: and immediately his feet and ankle bones received strength.

And he leaping up stood, and walked, and entered with them into the temple, walking, and leaping, and praising God.

And all the people saw him walking and praising God:

And they knew that it was he which sat for alms at the Beautiful gate of the temple: and they were filled with wonder and amazement at that which had happened to him."

ACTS

In his role as the Wayshower, Jesus revealed the fundamental truth that anyone who discerns the esoteric meaning of his teaching will also be able to perform the "works that I do. . .and [even] greater works than these shall he do." This prophetic declaration of the Master was not intended solely for the benefit of his immediate followers. This was a spiritual promise to men and women of all future generations. Any person who achieves an absolute recognition of his indwelling Christhood—a realization of his own divine *I*-dentity—must become a living transparency through which the harmony of God's perfect creation can manifest itself in the visible realm.

"And there sat a certain man at Lystra, impotent in his feet, being a cripple from his mother's womb, who never had walked:

The same heard Paul speak: who steadfastly beholding him, and perceiving that he had faith to be healed,

Said with a loud voice, 'Stand upright on thy feet.' And he leaped and walked."

ACTS

"And it came to pass, as Peter passed throughout all quarters, he came down also to the saints which dwelt at Lydda.

And there he found a certain man named Aeneas, which had kept his bed eight years, and was sick of the palsy.

And Peter said unto him, 'Aeneas, Jesus Christ maketh thee whole: arise, and make thy bed.' And he arose immediately."

ACTS

"And it came to pass, that the father of Publius lay sick of a fever and of a bloody flux: to whom Paul entered in, and prayed, and laid his hands on him, and healed him.

So when this was done, others also, which had diseases in the island, came, and were healed."

ACTS

"Wherefore, by their fruits ye shall know them."

CHRIST JESUS
As Recorded by MATTHEW

"And these signs shall follow them that believe; In my name shall they cast out devils; they shall speak with new tongues;

They shall take up serpents; and if they drink any deadly thing, it shall not hurt them; they shall lay hands on the sick, and they shall recover."

CHRIST JESUS
As Recorded by MARK

PROTECTION AND FREEDOM
("It Shall Not Come Nigh Thee")

"The Lord is my rock, and my fortress, and my deliverer;
The God of my rock; in Him will I trust: He is my shield
and the horn of my salvation, my high tower, and my refuge, my
saviour; Thou savest me from violence."

DAVID, The King
As Recorded in 2nd SAMUEL

"He that dwelleth in the secret place of the Most High shall
abide under the shadow of the Almighty.

I will say of the Lord, 'He is my refuge and my fortress: my
God; in Him will I trust.'

Surely He shall deliver thee from the snare of the fowler,
and from the noisome pestilence.

He shall cover thee with His feathers, and under His wings
shalt thou trust: His truth shall be thy shield and buckler.

Thou shalt not be afraid for the terror by night; nor for the
arrow that flieth by day;

Nor for the pestilence that walketh in darkness; nor for the
destruction that wasteth at noonday.

A thousand shall fall at thy side, and ten thousand at thy
right hand; but it shall not come nigh thee.

Because thou hast made the Lord, which is thy refuge, even
the Most High, thy habitation;

There shall no evil befall thee, neither shall any plague come
nigh thy dwelling."

PSALM 91

The scriptures of the world provide many examples of seemingly miraculous spiritual healings. And these same writings also promise that the "children of God" will be protected from most of the ills that flesh is heir to. But in almost every case, there is a condition attached to this promise of protection.

If we live exclusively as the "natural man"—if we accept an identity that is functioning independently from Divine Consciousness—we are not under the law of God and, for that reason, cannot be a beneficiary of the Scriptural guarantee of immunity.

The most basic precept of the ninety-first Psalm reveals that we must dwell in the constant realization of the Presence of God in order to be delivered from the ramifications of sin, disease and death.

This activity of "dwelling in the secret place of the Most High" requires a conscious effort on our part. We need to fully understand the mystical truth of Being and, then, we must devote several periods every day to recognizing our oneness with our Source. As we continue to follow this procedure, we will find less of the world's problems coming "nigh our dwelling place."

"Thou wilt keep him in perfect peace, whose mind is stayed on Thee: because he trusteth in Thee."

ISAIAH

"The Lord will perfect that which concerneth me."

PSALM 138

"No weapon that is formed against thee shall prosper."

ISAIAH

If we were to accept those Biblical passages literally, we might assume that God has the wherewithal to protect us from the negative events of "this world"—that God is aware of some impending danger that is about to come upon us and then, through an act of celestial intervention, prevents that occurrence from taking place. But that entire idea is based upon a faulty premise. It is predicated upon the belief that God is not infinite, and that this omnipresent Creator exists separate from His creation; it infers that God, the supremely perfect, immortal Being, has somehow created imperfection; it surmises that God not only is aware of evil but actually has created evil. And then because of some righteous prayers that we have uttered, the God Who is of "purer eyes than to behold evil" supposedly is going to enter the human scene and protect us from this "divinely-created evil."

In order to clarify this contradictory hypothesis, we must understand that the authors of these Biblical texts lived a long time ago, during an extremely primitive period in mankind's history. They wrote at a time when tradition and superstition were rampant. They had been influenced by numerous ancient legends that had been passed down from generation to generation, and their written manuscripts certainly reflected some of those external influences. Even those somewhat enlightened men who were in direct communication with God—those who actually received revelation—were still presenting the divine impartations from their personal perspective. Their writings had to be contemporary with the times in which they lived; so even though the Divine Consciousness was unfolding and disclosing Itself *in* and *as* absolute Truth, those learned men of antiquity were perceiving this holy revelation through limited vision: through their own three-dimensional, finite sense of understanding.

But today, because of many succeeding generations of enlightenment, because many illumined men and women have glimpsed the undisputable fact that God is infinite— omnipresent, omniscient, and omnipotent—the unadulterated truth of Being can finally be given to all mankind. This higher Truth has, in fact, always been an intrinsic element of the Scriptural writings. But in the ancient manuscripts, the esoteric meaning of the message has been veiled; it has been hidden from view and can be discerned only as consciousness is raised to a higher level of awareness and spiritual perception. Accordingly, this ultimate revelation of Truth discloses that, because of the allness of God, there is no evil, there is no error, and there are no negative circumstances that can actually exist in the real life-experience of the begotten child of God. As a consequence, we don't need to be protected from the wrath of God. We need protection only from our unwitting acquiescence to the belief in two powers.

"Know ye not, that to whom ye yield yourselves servants to obey, his servants ye are to whom ye obey...

And be not conformed to this world: but be ye transformed by the renewing of your mind, that ye may prove what is that good, and acceptable, and perfect, will of God."

PAUL
To the ROMANS

"No man can serve two masters: for either he will hate the one, and love the other; or else he will hold to the one, and despise the other. Ye cannot serve God and mammon."

CHRIST JESUS
As Recorded by MATTHEW

"Choose you this day whom ye will serve. . .but as for me and my house, we will serve the Lord.

Be strong and of a good courage; be not afraid, neither be thou dismayed: for the Lord thy God is with thee withersoever thou goest."

JOSHUA

"Put not your trust in princes, nor in the son of man, in whom there is no help."

PSALM 146

"I will lift up mine eyes unto the hills, from whence cometh my help.

My help cometh from the Lord, which made heaven and earth.

The Lord shall preserve thee from all evil: He shall preserve thy soul."

PSALM 121

The first step in doing protective work for ourselves and our loved ones is to realize that, since God is the only power, we need not fear "man, whose breath is in his nostrils"—his false hypotheses about life, his germ theories, his unwarranted fears, nor his acceptance of the belief in two powers. All of these are mere human concepts and cannot affect the spiritual child of God, that person "who has his being in Christ."

God is omnipotent, the only power that exists. And since God is Spirit, spiritual power must be the governing force in our life. Because of the omnipotence of God, we cannot be intimidated by any forms of temporal power, whether these appear as alien armies, power-mad dictators, totalitarian governments, or "spiritual wickedness in high places."

"Thou couldest have no power at all against me, except it were given thee from above."

CHRIST JESUS
As Recorded by JOHN

"Now the Philistines gathered together their armies to battle...

And Saul and the men of Israel were gathered together...

And the Philistines stood on a mountain on the one side, and Israel stood on a mountain on the other side: and there was a valley between them.

And there went out a champion out of the camp of the Philistines, named Goliath, of Gath, whose height was six cubits and a span.

And he stood and cried unto the armies of Israel, and said unto them, 'Why are ye come out to set your battle in array? Am not I a Philistine, and ye servants to Saul? Choose you a man for you, and let him come down to me.

'If he be able to fight with me, and to kill me, then will we be your servants: but if I prevail against him, and kill him, then shall ye be our servants, and serve us.'

And the Philistine said, 'I defy the armies of Israel this day; give me a man, that we may fight together.'

When Saul and all Israel heard those words of the Philistine, they were dismayed, and greatly afraid.

Now David was the son of the Ephrathite of Bethlehem-judah, whose name was Jesse; and he had eight sons...

And David was the youngest: and the three eldest followed Saul.

Now Saul, and they, and all the men of Israel, were in the valley of Elah, fighting with the Philistines.

And David rose up early in the morning, and left the sheep with a keeper, and took, and went, as Jesse had commanded him; and he came to the trench, as the host was going forth to the fight, and shouted for the battle.

And David left his carriage in the hand of the keeper of the carriage, and ran into the army, and came and saluted his brethren.

And as he talked with them, behold, there came up the champion, the Philistine of Gath, Goliath by name, out of the armies of the Philistines, and spake according to the same words: and David heard them.

And all the men of Israel, when they saw the man, fled from him, and were sore afraid.

And David said to Saul, 'Let no man's heart fail because of him; thy servant will go and fight with this Philistine.'

And Saul said to David, 'Thou art not able to go against this Philistine to fight with him: for thou art but a youth, and he a man of war from his youth.'

David said moreover, 'The Lord that delivered me out of the paw of the lion, and out of the paw of the bear, He will deliver me out of the hand of this Philistine.' And Saul said unto David, 'Go, and the Lord be with thee.'

And Saul armed David with his armour, and he put an helmet of brass upon his head; also he armed him with a coat of mail.

And David girded his sword upon his armour, and he assayed to go; for he had not proved it. And David said unto Saul, 'I cannot go with these; for I have not proved them.' And David put them off him.

And he took his staff in his hand, and chose him five smooth stones out of the brook, and put them in a shepherd's bag which he had, even in a scrip; and his sling was in his hand: and he drew near to the Philistine.

And the Philistine came on and drew near unto David; and the man that bare the shield went before him.

And when the Philistine looked about, and saw David, he disdained him: for he was but a youth, and ruddy, and of a fair countenance.

And the Philistine said unto David, 'Come to me, and I will give thy flesh unto the fowls of the air, and to the beasts of the field.'

Then said David to the Philistine, 'Thou comest to me with a sword, and with a spear, and with a shield: but I come to thee in the name of the Lord of hosts, the God of the armies of Israel, Whom thou hast defied.

'This day will the Lord deliver thee into mine hand; and I will smite thee, and take thine head from thee; and I will give the carcases of the host of the Philistines this day unto the fowls of the air, and to the wild beasts of the earth; that all the earth may know that there is a God in Israel.

'And all this assembly shall know that the Lord saveth not with sword and spear: for the battle is the Lord's and He will give you into our hands.'

And it came to pass, when the Philistine arose, and came and drew nigh to meet David, that David hasted, and ran toward the army to meet the Philistine.

And David put his hand in his bag, and took thence a stone, and slang it, and smote the Philistine in his forehead, that the stone sunk into his forehead; and he fell upon his face to the earth.

So David prevailed over the Philistine with a sling and with a stone, and smote the Philistine, and slew him; but there was no sword in the hand of David."

1st SAMUEL

Throughout Biblical history, it is recorded that those who lived in the conscious realization of the omnipresence and omnipotence of God were protected from the temporal evil forces of "this world." Every negative circumstance that comes into our life can be nullified by the recognition of the non-power of anything appearing in the three-dimensional realm of cause and effect. "One on God's side is a majority." When we accept our unity with the Infinite Invisible, we can face all the Goliaths of this world with the sacred assurance that, in reality, no form of evil can actually "come nigh our dwelling place."

"Nebuchadnezzar the king made an image of gold, whose height was three-score cubits, and the breadth thereof six cubits: he set it up in the plain of Dura, in the province of Babylon.

Wherefore at that time certain Chaldeans came near, and accused the Jews.

They spake and said to the king Nebuchadnezzar, 'O King, live for ever.

'Thou, O King, hast made a decree, that every man that shall hear the sound of the cornet, flute, harp, sackbut, psaltery, and dulcimer, and all kinds of musick, shall fall down and worship the golden image:

'And whoso falleth not down and worshippeth, that he should be cast into the midst of a burning fiery furnace.

'There are certain Jews whom thou hast set over the affairs of the province of Babylon, Shadrach, Meshach, and Abednego; these men, O King, have not regarded thee: they serve not thy gods, nor worship the golden image which thou hast set up.'

Then Nebuchadnezzar in his rage and fury commanded to bring Shadrach, Meshach, and Abednego. Then they brought these men before the king.

Nebuchadnezzar spake and said unto them, 'Is it true, O Shadrach, Meshach, and Abednego, do not ye serve my gods, nor worship the golden image which I have set up?

'... but if ye worship not, ye shall be cast the same hour into the midst of a burning fiery furnace; and who is that God that shall deliver you out of my hands?'

Shadrach, Meshach, and Abednego, answered and said to the king, 'O Nebuchadnezzar, we are not careful to answer thee in this matter.

'If it be so, our God whom we serve is able to deliver us from the burning fiery furnace, and he will deliver us out of thine hand, O King.

'But if not, be it known unto thee, O King, that we will not serve thy gods, nor worship the golden image which thou hast set up.'

Then was Nebuchadnezzar full of fury, and the form of his visage was changed against Shadrach, Meshach, and Abednego: therefore he spake, and commanded that they should heat the furnace one seven times more than it was wont to be heated.

And he commanded the most mighty men that were in his army to bind Shadrach, Meshach, and Abednego, and to cast them into the burning fiery furnace.

Then these men were bound in their coats, their hosen, and their hats, and their other garments, and were cast into the midst of the burning fiery furnace.

Therefore because the King's commandment was urgent, and the furnace exceeding hot, the flame of the fire slew those men that took up Shadrach, Meshach, and Abednego.

And these three men, Shadrach, Meshach, and Abednego, fell down bound into the midst of the burning fiery furnace.

Then Nebuchadnezzar the King was [astonished], and rose up in haste, and spake, and said unto his counsellors, 'Did not we cast three men bound into the midst of the fire?' They answered and said unto the King, 'True, O King.'

He answered and said, 'Lo, I see four men loose, walking in the midst of the fire, and they have no hurt; and the form of the fourth is like the Son of God.'

Then Nebuchadnezzar came near to the mouth of the burning fiery furnace, and spake, and said, 'Shadrach, Meshach, and Abednego, ye servants of the most high God, come forth, and come hither.' Then Shadrach, Meshach, and Abednego, came forth of the midst of the fire.

And the princes, governors, and captains, and the king's counsellors, being gathered together, saw these men, upon whose bodies the fire had no power, nor was an hair of their head singed, neither were their coats changed, nor the smell of fire had passed on them.

Then Nebuchadnezzar spake, and said, 'Blessed be the God of Shadrach, Meshach, and Abednego, Who hath sent His angel, and delivered His servants that trusted in Him, and have changed the king's word, and yielded their bodies, that they might not serve nor worship any god, except their own God.'"

DANIEL

"Thou shalt have no other gods before Me."

EXODUS

The first commandment of the Mosaic Decalogue dissuades us from so much more than just the mere worshipping of golden idols.

God is the only Life, the one omnipotent Consciousness. So if we are acknowledging any life other than the Life that is God, if we are believing that there is power in matter or in any other effect, if we are accepting reality or substance in anything other than this one omnipresent Being, we are breaking that first commandment.

However, if we refuse to bow down and worship false gods—if we refuse to believe in the illusory, temporal powers of "this world"—we are adhering to our highest sense of right. By virtue of that activity, we are loving God with all our heart, soul, and mind and, then, are consciously placing ourselves under the law of God.

As a result of that act of commitment, we are granted immunity from the false beliefs of mankind. Then, as in the Biblical example of the three Hebrews, we, too, could be cast into our "fiery furnace" and would be able to step right out of it unscathed. Our understanding, acknowledgement, and realization of the allness of God can sustain us through any negative human circumstance.

"In God I will praise His word, in God I have put my trust; I will not fear what flesh can do unto me.

In God have I put my trust: I will not be afraid what man can do unto me."

PSALM 56

"The Lord is on my side; I will not fear: what can man do unto me?

It is better to trust in the Lord than to put confidence in princes."

PSALM 118

Along with being protected from the evil circumstances of humanhood, we also will find our freedom—freedom from false beliefs, freedom from domination by any other person or ideology, and freedom to live our life with dominion over all things.

"In Thy presence is fulness of joy."

PSALM 16

"Where the Spirit of the Lord is, there is liberty."

PAUL
To the CORINTHIANS

"There is neither Jew nor Greek, there is neither bond nor free, there is neither male nor female: for ye are all one in Christ Jesus.

Stand fast therefore in the liberty wherewith Christ hath made us free, and be not entangled again with the yoke of bondage."

> *PAUL*
> *To the GALATIANS*

Because of the infinitude of God's Being, it is absolutely impossible for us to be removed from the Divine Presence. There is no place where we can go in which we actually are separated from the life and love of God. Only in belief can such separation occur; only when we have accepted an identity apart from God-Consciousness can we even mentally entertain such a false sense of separation. But if we practice right-identification—if we consciously dwell in the "secret place of the Most High"—we are exercising our God-given dominion over all circumstances and situations. This, then, is our guarantee of immunity from the seeming problems of "this world." And, as the Psalmist has assured us: "It shall not come nigh thee. . . ."

"God is our refuge and strength, a very present help in trouble.

Therefore will not we fear, though the earth be removed, and though the mountains be carried into the midst of the sea;

Though the waters thereof roar and be troubled, though the mountains shake with the swelling thereof.

There is a river, the streams whereof shall make glad the city of God, the holy place of the tabernacles of the Most High.

God is in the midst of her; she shall not be moved: God shall help her, and that right early.

The heathen raged, the kingdoms were moved: He uttered His voice, the earth melted.

'Be still, and know that I am God...'

The Lord of hosts is with us; the God of Jacob is our refuge."

PSALM 46

"The Lord is my shepherd; I shall not want.

He maketh me to lie down in green pastures: He leadeth me beside the still waters.

He restoreth my soul: He leadeth me in the paths of righteousness for His name's sake.

Yea, though I walk through the valley of the shadow of death, I will fear no evil: for Thou art with me; Thy rod and Thy staff they comfort me,

Thou preparest a table before me in the presence of mine enemies: Thou anointest my head with oil; my cup runneth over.

Surely goodness and mercy shall follow me all the days of my life: and I will dwell in the house of the Lord for ever."

PSALM 23

REVELATION
("The Word Made Flesh")

"Know therefore this day, and consider it in thine heart, that the Lord He is God in heaven above, and upon the earth beneath: there is none else."

MOSES
As Recorded in DEUTERONOMY

"Is there a God beside Me? Yea, there is no God; I know not any.
My glory will I not give to another."

ISAIAH

"But as it is written, Eye hath not seen, nor ear heard, neither have entered into the heart of man, the things which God hath prepared for them that love Him.
But God hath revealed them unto us by His Spirit: for the Spirit searcheth all things, yea, the deep things of God.
For what man knoweth the things of a man, save the spirit of man which is in him? Even so the things of God knoweth no man, but the Spirit of God."

PAUL
To the CORINTHIANS

"Great is our Lord, and of great power: His understanding is infinite."

PSALM 147

God, the one universal Consciousness, is omniscient! Therefore, all wisdom, all knowledge, all intelligence—the multitudinous facets of absolute Truth—already exist in this Divine Consciousness.

God also is omnipresent! And because this everpresent Being fills all space, Consciousness is the essence and substance of all that Is. Therefore, man does not exist external to God-Consciousness. Spiritual man is begotten of the Father. God expresses Himself in a uniquely exclusive way *as* the individual identity of each one of us. But because we have accepted a belief in a personal ego—a mortal selfhood that is separated from its Source—we have abandoned our divine heritage and, according to physical sense testimony, appear to be functioning as a finite and limited human being.

However, in our personal quest to return to our primal state of consciousness—that state in which we had a full awareness of our Christ-identity—we reach a specific point in time when we have our spiritual awakening. Then, after that first moment of illumination, we begin to study and practice certain metaphysical principles as we strive to acquire an intellectual understanding of the Letter of Truth.

Unfortunately, at that point in our unfoldment, many of us lose our way as we become satisfied just to read and hear words about Truth. Others fail to catch the vision that they already have oneness with God as an inherent characteristic of their own being. As a result of these factors, most of us then begin looking outside ourselves, hoping that some enlightened human teacher can give us eternal life and the inspired Word of God.

"To whom shall we go, thou hast the words of eternal life?"

JOHN

"My words shall not pass away."

CHRIST JESUS
As Recorded by LUKE

"The words that I speak unto you, they are spirit, and they are life."

CHRIST JESUS
As Recorded by JOHN

The words spoken by Jesus and by other illumined revelators of the past can guide us on our spiritual journey. But even though their teachings may live on for centuries, eventually those teachers *must* and *do* leave the human scene. For that reason, every true spiritual teacher will direct his students' attention and worship away from himself, the teacher, thus enabling each person to ultimately achieve his own individual God-experience and personal revelation of absolute Truth.

"I will pray the Father, and He shall give you another Comforter, that He may abide with you for ever;
Even the Spirit of truth; whom the world cannot receive, because it seeth Him not, neither knoweth Him: but ye know Him; for He dwelleth with you, and shall be in you.

I will not leave you comfortless...

But the Comforter, which is the Holy Ghost, whom the Father will send in my name, He shall teach you all things and bring all things to your remembrance, whatsoever I have said unto you.

Peace I leave with you, my peace I give unto you: not as the world giveth, give I unto you. Let not your heart be troubled, neither let it be afraid.

Nevertheless I tell you the truth; It is expedient for you that I go away: for if I go not away, the Comforter will not come unto you; but if I depart, I will send Him unto you.

Howbeit when He, the Spirit of truth, is come, He will guide you into all truth."

CHRIST JESUS
As Recorded by JOHN

"Strait is the gate, and narrow is the way, which leadeth unto life, and few there be that find it."

CHRIST JESUS
As Recorded by MATTHEW

As we grow in spiritual wisdom, we realize that something more than just a human teacher is needed. And, even though we are grateful to our spiritual guides, we eventually seek an even higher revelation of Truth—a revelation that transcends the mere mental processes of our thinking mind. This greater unfoldment takes place when we achieve a mystical union with the Divine Consciousness, and then the immortal and pure Word of God can be revealed within us.

"In the beginning was the Word, and the Word was with God, and the Word was God.

And the Word was made flesh and dwelt among us."

JOHN

"Now we have received, not the spirit of the world, but the Spirit which is of God; that we might know the things that are freely given to us of God.

Which things also we speak, not in the words which man's wisdom teacheth, but which the Holy Ghost teacheth; comparing spiritual things with spiritual.

But the natural man receiveth not the things of the Spirit of God: for they are foolishness unto him: neither can he know them, because they are spiritually discerned."

PAUL
To the CORINTHIANS

"For the Lord giveth wisdom: out of His mouth cometh knowledge and understanding.

Happy is the man that findeth wisdom, and the man that getteth understanding.

Wisdom is the principal thing; therefore get wisdom: and with all thy getting get understanding."

PROVERBS

"*For God speaketh once, yea twice, yet man perceiveth it not.*

But there is a Spirit in man: and the inspiration of the Almighty giveth them understanding."

ELIHU, the son of
Barachel the Buzite
As Recorded by JOB

After our spiritual awakening, we quickly develop a seemingly unquenchable thirst for more knowledge. But because the counterfeit laws and false beliefs of "this world" have been ingrained in us over a period of many lifetimes, we often have difficulty in breaking through the barriers of material sense. In fact, it is virtually impossible for a human being to follow the "strait and narrow way" of Truth. Paul tells us that "the natural man receiveth not the things of God." Yet even while we are functioning in this "man of earth" state, we must begin our search for God. But as we embark upon this spiritual journey, we soon realize that, ultimately, we must surrender our old beliefs about life and rise to a new dimension of mystical consciousness.

"*Thus saith the Lord, 'Let not the wise man glory in his wisdom...*

'*But let him that glorieth glory in this, that he understandeth and knoweth Me.*'"

JEREMIAH

"*Give instruction to a wise man, and he will be yet wiser: teach a just man, and he will increase in learning.*

The fear of the Lord is the beginning of wisdom: and the knowledge of the Holy is understanding."

PROVERBS

"For since the beginning of the world men have not heard, nor perceived by the ear, neither hath the eye seen, O God, beside Thee, what He hath prepared for him that waiteth for Him."

ISAIAH

"And [Jesus] said unto them, 'How is it that ye do not understand?
'Having eyes, see ye not? and having ears, hear ye not?'"

CHRIST JESUS
As Recorded by MARK

Spiritual perception is a quality that each of us needs to develop. That is what Jesus was alluding to when he said: "Having eyes, see ye not? and having ears, hear ye not?" The Master knew that divine Truth cannot be perceived through our human mind or through our five physical senses. At most, we can use these human faculties to become aware of the Letter of Truth. But in order to have a direct revelation of the inspired Word of God, we must perfect our spiritual faculties. The enlightened Apostle Paul recognized the futility of merely cultivating the human intellect:

"Not that we are sufficient of ourselves to think any thing as of ourselves; but our sufficiency is of God;
Who also hath made us able ministers of the new testament; not of the letter, but of the spirit: for the letter killeth, but the spirit giveth life."

PAUL
To the CORINTHIANS

"For there is no respect of persons with God.
Yea, let God be true, but every man a liar."

PAUL
To the ROMANS

"He that hath an ear, let him hear what the Spirit saith...
'To him that overcometh will I give to eat of the hidden manna,
and will give him a white stone, and in the stone a new name
written, which no man knoweth saving he that receiveth it.'"

REVELATION

"Trust in the Lord with all thine heart; and lean not unto
thine own understanding.
In all thy ways acknowledge Him, and He shall direct thy
paths."

PROVERBS

"Man shall not live by bread alone, but by every word that
proceedeth out of the mouth of God."

CHRIST JESUS
As Recorded by MATTHEW

As we "die" to our false sense of self and put off the "old
[concept of] man," we are taking the first steps in preparing
ourselves to become receptive to "every word that proceedeth

out of the mouth of God." Many people, while living exclusively in their "natural man" state of consciousness, find it quite difficult to give up their worldly desires and long-standing false beliefs. In fact, for a good number of these people, the first introduction to Truth is somewhat shocking to the intellect and brings forth a negative reaction.

"And I went unto the angel, and said unto him, 'Give me the little book.' And he said unto me, 'Take it, and eat it up; and it shall make thy belly bitter, but it shall be in thy mouth sweet as honey.'"

REVELATION

"No man putteth a piece of new cloth unto an old garment, for that which is put in to fill it up taketh from the garment, and the (tear) is made worse.

Neither do men put new wine into old bottles: else the bottles break, and the wine runneth out, and the bottles perish: but they put new wine into new bottles, and both are preserved.

CHRIST JESUS
As Recorded by MATTHEW

While some students discover that the first taste of Truth "makes the belly bitter," others acknowledge an instantaneous agreement with the spiritual principles. But whatever our initial reaction may be, as seekers after Truth we must undergo a radical change of consciousness. We must literally be reborn of the Spirit. As "new wine cannot be put into old bottles," neither can spiritual reality be discerned by someone who is functioning at the level of finite and limited human perception.

"*Verily I say unto you, Whosoever shall not receive the kingdom of God as a little child shall in no wise enter therein.*"

CHRIST JESUS
As Recorded by LUKE

"*It is written in the prophets, 'And they shall be all taught of God.'*"

CHRIST JESUS
As Recorded by JOHN

"*That which may be known of God is manifest in them; for God hath shewed it unto them.*

For the invisible things of Him from the creation of the world are clearly seen, being understood by the things that are made, even His eternal power and Godhead."

PAUL
To the ROMANS

As we develop a child-like innocence and relinquish the false conditioning of our human mind, we become capable of surrendering to the fourth-dimensional reality of Divine Consciousness. Then this omniscient Being functions as our individual consciousness and, in that state of oneness, we truly "shall be all taught of God."

"He performeth the thing that is appointed for me."

JOB

"The Word of God is quick and powerful and sharper than any two-edged sword."

HEBREWS

"For (now) we know in part, and we prophesy in part.

But when that which is perfect is come, then that which is in part shall be done away.

When I was a child, I spake as a child, I understood as a child, I thought as a child: but when I became a man, I put away childish things.

For now we see through a glass, darkly; but then face to face: now I know in part; but then shall I know even as also I am known."

PAUL
To the CORINTHIANS

"Whereas I was blind, now I see."

JOHN

TRANSITION
("The Last Enemy")

"And Moses was an hundred and twenty years old when he died: his eye was not dim, nor his natural force abated."

DEUTERONOMY

"'For I have no pleasure in the death of him that dieth,' saith the Lord God: 'wherefore, turn yourselves, and live ye.'"

EZEKIEL

According to world belief, every human being has been born into a physical body and, eventually, will die out of that body. But that limited sense of life does not evince ultimate reality. Humanhood is a false concept about our real identity. In truth, each one of us is the spiritual individualization of the Divine Consciousness and, therefore, we share in the God-Life. Hence our life is eternal and cannot ultimately end in death.

"Lord, Thou hast been our dwelling place in all generations.
Before the mountains were brought forth, or ever Thou hadst formed the earth and the world, even from everlasting to everlasting."

PSALM 90

"Whither shall I go from Thy spirit? Or whither shall I flee from Thy presence?

If I ascend up into heaven, Thou art there: if I make my bed in hell, behold, Thou art there.

If I take the wings of the morning, and dwell in the uttermost parts of the sea;

Even there shall Thy hand lead me, and Thy right hand shall hold me."

PSALM 139

"While [Jesus] yet spake, there cometh one from the ruler of the synagogue's house, saying to him, 'Thy daughter is dead; trouble not the Master.'

But when Jesus heard it, he answered him, saying, 'Fear not: believe only, and she shall be made whole.'

And when he came into the house, he suffered no man to go in, save Peter, and James, and John, and the father and the mother of the maiden.

And all wept, and bewailed her: but he said, 'Weep not; she is not dead, but sleepeth.'

And they laughed him to scorn, knowing that she was dead.

And he put them all out, and took her by the hand, and called, saying, 'Maid, arise.'

And her spirit came again, and she arose straightway: and he commanded to give her meat.

And her parents were astonished: but he charged them that they should tell no man what was done.

LUKE.

In the healing ministry of Christ Jesus, there are several recorded instances in which he was confronted with the illusion of death. But instead of accepting those false pictures, the Master faced up to each erroneous appearance with an abiding conviction that the Life that is God is the only life. Where others saw mortality and death, Jesus beheld eternal existence. Functioning perpetually in a state of oneness with the Father, he was the Christ of God; and from that illumined vantage point, the Master literally became a transparency through which the perfection and harmony of God's immaculate creation could be manifested in the visible realm.

"And it came to pass the day after, that [Jesus] went into a city called Nain; and many of his disciples went with him, and much people.

Now when he came nigh to the gate of the city, behold, there was a dead man carried out, the only son of his mother, and she was a widow: and much people of the city was with her.

And when the Lord saw her, he had compassion on her, and said unto her, 'Weep not.'

And he came and touched the bier: and they that bare him stood still. And [Jesus] said, 'Young man, I say unto thee, Arise.'

And he that was dead sat up, and began to speak. And he delivered him to his mother.

LUKE

"For since by man came death, by man came also the resurrection of the dead.

For as in Adam all die, even so in Christ shall all be made alive.

PAUL
To the CORINTHIANS

"Now a certain man was sick, named Lazarus, of Bethany, the town of Mary and her sister Martha.

(It was that Mary which anointed the Lord with ointment, and wiped his feet with her hair, whose brother Lazarus was sick.)

Therefore, his sisters sent unto [Jesus], saying, 'Lord, behold, he whom thou lovest is sick.'

When Jesus heard that, he said, 'This sickness is not unto death, but for the glory of God, that the Son of God might be glorified thereby.'

Now Jesus loved Martha, and her sister, and Lazarus.

When he had heard therefore that he was sick, he abode two days still in the same place where he was.

Then after that saith he to his disciples, 'Let us go into Judea again.'

... And after that he saith unto them, 'Our friend Lazarus sleepeth; but I go, that I may awake him out of sleep.'

Then said his disciples, 'Lord, if he sleep, he shall do well.'

Howbeit Jesus spake of his death: but they thought that he had spoken of taking of rest in sleep.

Then said Jesus unto them plainly, 'Lazarus is dead.

'And I am glad for your sakes that I was not there, to the intent ye may believe; nevertheless let us go unto him.'

Then when Jesus came, he found that he had lain in the grave four days already.

Now Bethany was nigh unto Jerusalem, about fifteen furlongs off:

And many of the Jews came to Martha and Mary, to comfort them concerning their brother.

Then Martha, as soon as she heard that Jesus was coming, went and met him: but Mary sat still in the house.

Then said Martha unto Jesus, 'Lord, if thou hadst been here, my brother had not died.

'But I know, that even now, whatsoever thou wilt ask of God, God will give it thee.'

Jesus saith unto her, 'Thy brother shall rise again.'

Martha saith unto him, 'I know that he shall rise again in the resurrection at the last day.'

Jesus said unto her, 'I am the resurrection, and the life: he that believeth in me, though he were dead, yet shall he live:

'And whosoever liveth and believeth in me shall never die. Believest thou this?'

She saith unto him, 'Yea, Lord: I believe that thou art the Christ, the Son of God, which should come into the world.'

And when she had so said, she went her way, and called Mary her sister secretly, saying, 'The Master is come, and calleth for thee.'

As soon as [Mary] heard that, she arose quickly, and came unto him.

Now Jesus was not yet come into the town, but was in that place where Martha met him.

The Jews then which were with her in the house, and comforted her, when they saw Mary, that she rose up hastily and went out, followed her, saying, 'She goeth unto the grave to weep there.'

Then when Mary was come where Jesus was, and saw him, she fell down at his feet, saying unto him, 'Lord, if thou hadst been here, my brother had not died.'

When Jesus therefore saw her weeping, and the Jews also weeping which came with her, he groaned in the spirit, and was troubled,

And said, 'Where have ye laid him?' They said unto him, 'Lord, come and see.'

Jesus wept.

Then said the Jews, 'Behold how he loved him!'

And some of them said, 'Could not this man, which opened the eyes of the blind, have caused that even this man should not have died?'

Jesus therefore again groaning in himself cometh to the grave. It was a cave, and a stone lay upon it.

Jesus said, 'Take ye away the stone.' Martha, the sister of him that was dead, saith unto him, 'Lord, by this time he stinketh: for he hath been dead four days.'

Jesus saith unto her, 'Said I not unto thee, that, if thou wouldest believe, thou shouldest see the glory of God?'

Then they took away the stone from the place where the dead was laid. And Jesus lifted up his eyes, and said, 'Father, I thank Thee that Thou hast heard me.

'And I knew that Thou hearest me always: but because of the people which stand by I said it, that they may believe that Thou hast sent me.'

And when he thus had spoken, he cried with a loud voice, 'Lazarus, come forth.'

And he that was dead came forth, bound hand and foot with graveclothes: and his face was bound about with a napkin. Jesus saith unto them, 'Loose him, and let him go.'

JOHN

"O death, where is thy sting? O grave, where is thy victory?

But some man will say, 'How are the dead raised up? and with what body do they come?'

Thou fool, that which thou sowest is not quickened [made alive], except it die:

And that which thou sowest, thou sowest not that body that shall be...

But God giveth it a body as it hath pleased Him, and to every seed His own body.

So also is the resurrection of the dead. It is sown in corruption; it is raised in incorruption:

It is sown in dishonour; it is raised in glory: it is sown in weakness; it is raised in power:

It is sown a natural body; it is raised a spiritual body. There is a natural body, and there is a spiritual body.

And so it is written, The first man Adam was made a living soul; the last Adam was made a quickening spirit.

The first man is of the earth, earthy: the second man is the Lord from heaven.

As is the earthy, such are they also that are earthy: and as is the heavenly, such are they also that are heavenly.

And as we have borne the image of the earthy, we shall also bear the image of the heavenly.

Now this I say, brethren, that flesh and blood cannot inherit the kingdom of God; neither doth corruption inherit incorruption.

For this corruptible must put on incorruption, and this mortal must put on immortality.

So when this corruptible shall have put on incorruption, and this mortal shall have put on immortality, then shall be brought to pass the saying that is written: Death is swallowed up in victory.

The last enemy that shall be destroyed is death."

PAUL
To the CORINTHIANS

The illusion of death can appear only in the experience of that person who has accepted the claim that he is the progeny of Adam and Eve—that person who is "of the earth, earthy." However, once we discover our real identity as the spiritual offspring of God, we live in a state of eternal bliss as the "second man who shall bear the image of the heavenly." The phenomenon of immortal life is our divine destiny. But in order for us to enjoy the fruitage of this sacred birthright, we must accept the fundamental truth that God actually is our life. Functioning from that enlightened standpoint, we will never again fear the temporal powers of "this world" and we will be able to face even "the last enemy" with the implicit assurance that our real spiritual life in God-Consciousness will continue forever.

"When the morning was come, all the chief priests and elders of the people took counsel against Jesus to put him to death:

And when they had bound him, they led him away, and delivered him to Pontius Pilate the governor.

And Pilate asked him, 'Art thou the King of the Jews?' And [Jesus] answering said unto him, 'Thou sayest it.'

And the chief priests accused him of many things: but he answered nothing.

Then saith Pilate unto him, 'Speakest thou not unto me? Knowest thou not that I have power to crucify thee, and have power to release thee?'

Jesus answered, 'Thou couldest have no power at all against me, except it were given thee from above...'

And Pilate, when he had called together the chief priests and the rulers and the people,

Said unto them, 'Ye have brought this man unto me, as one that perverteth the people: and, behold, I, having examined him before you, have found no fault in this man touching those things whereof ye accuse him:

'I will therefore chastise him, and release him.'

And they cried out all at once, saying, 'Away with this man...'

Pilate therefore, willing to release Jesus, spake again to them.

But they cried, saying, 'Crucify him, crucify him.'

And he said unto them the third time, 'Why, what evil hath he done? I have found no cause of death in him: I will therefore chastise him, and let him go.'

And they were instant with loud voices, requiring that he might be crucified. And the voices of them and of the chief priests prevailed.

And Pilate gave sentence that it should be as they required.

Then delivered he him therefore unto them to be crucified. And they took Jesus, and led him away.

And he bearing his cross went forth into a place called 'the place of a skull,' which is called in the Hebrew 'Golgotha':

And it was the third hour, and they crucified him.

And with him they crucify two thieves; the one on his right hand, and the other on his left.

And when the sixth hour was come, there was darkness over the whole land until the ninth hour.

And when Jesus had cried with a loud voice, he said, 'Father, into Thy hands I commend my spirit:' and having said thus, he gave up the ghost.

And, behold, there was a man named Joseph, a counsellor; and he was a good man, and a just:

...He was of Arimathœa, a city of the Jews: who also himself waited for the kingdom of God.

This man went unto Pilate, and begged the body of Jesus. Then Pilate commanded the body to be delivered.

And when Joseph had taken the body, he wrapped it in a clean linen cloth,

And laid it in his own new tomb, which he had hewn out in the rock: and he rolled a great stone to the door of the sepulchre, and departed.

And when the sabbath was past, Mary Magdalene, and Mary the mother of James, and Salome, had bought sweet spices, that they might come and anoint him.

And very early in the morning the first day of the week, they came unto the sepulchre at the rising of the sun.

And they said among themselves, 'Who shall roll us away the stone from the door of the sepulchre?'

And when they looked, they saw that the stone was rolled away: for it was very great.

And entering into the sepulchre, they saw a young man sitting on the right side, clothed in a long white garment; and they were affrighted.

And he saith unto them, 'Be not affrighted: Ye seek Jesus of Nazareth, which was crucified: he is risen; he is not here: behold the place where they laid him.'"

MATTHEW, MARK
LUKE and JOHN

"Destroy this temple, and in three days I will raise it up."

CHRIST JESUS
As Recorded by JOHN

Through his crucifixion and resurrection, the Master confirmed the immortal nature of life. Despite the world's belief that it had the ability to destroy his body and take his life, Jesus realized that, as the Christ of God, he had all power within his own consciousness. Having full cognizance of his oneness with God, this illumined Hebrew rabbi became our Wayshower as he demonstrated the fruitage of a life lived solely as an instrument through which the power and presence of God could be expressed.

Following the Master's remarkable example, we, too, can face any negative circumstances in our life, knowing that our real Christ-consciousness can resurrect and restore our business, our family, our home, our body—even "the years that the locust hath eaten."

"By faith, Enoch was translated that he should not see death; and was not found, because God had translated him."

HEBREWS

"And it came to pass, as they still went on, and talked, that, behold, there appeared a chariot of fire, and horses of fire, and parted them both asunder; and Elijah went up by a whirlwind into heaven."

2nd KINGS

While the experience of physical death seems to be a necessary step for most people, it is possible to go through a transition out of the flesh without being subjected to the traditional human processes. Both Enoch and Elijah were translated and did not leave their bodies behind.   Similarly, after his resurrection from his tomb, Jesus' work on this plane of existence was finished. And since he had risen, by that time, to an absolute state of conscious oneness with God, he then was able to experience a complete ascension above all finite human concepts.

"Afterward, he appeared unto the eleven as they sat at meat, and upbraided them with their unbelief and hardness of heart, because they believed not them which had seen him after he was risen.

Then opened he their understanding, that they might understand the scriptures.

And he led them out as far as to Bethany, and he lifted up his hands, and blessed them.

And it came to pass, while he blessed them, he was parted from them, and carried up into heaven."

MARK and LUKE

As each one of us comes into the full realization of our Christhood, we become capable of achieving total oneness with our Source. In that state of illumination, we rise into the fourth-dimensional reality of God-Consciousness and then, like the Master, we, too, will overcome even the "last enemy."

"For I am persuaded, that neither death, nor life, nor angels, nor principalities, nor powers, nor things present, nor things to come,

Nor height, nor depth, nor any other creature, shall be able to separate us from the love of God."

PAUL
To the ROMANS